Heaven and Hell

Let it be considered that if our lives ben't a journey to heaven they will be a journey to hell.

From a sermon on Heb. 11:13, 14, "This life ought so to be spent by us as to be only a journey towards heaven" (p. 2), Sept. 1733. At Boston, Oct. 1753, Stockbridge Indians. Preached at New Haven. Hickman, II, 243f.; Worcester, rev., IV, 573f., p. 33.

Jonathan Edwards

on

Heaven and Hell

by

Dr. John H. Gerstner

Soli Deo Gloria Publications
. . . for instruction in righteousness . . .

Soli Deo Gloria Publications
P. O. Box 451, Morgan, PA 15064
(412) 221-1901/FAX 221-1902

*

*

ISBN 1-57358-088-0

Preface

We read that God is love. The saints shall enjoy him when all flaming out in love.

And as God is love so also is he wrath. Hatred and wrath against the ungodliness and unrighteousness of men. And the wicked in hell shall be acquainted with him and have to do with him all excited and appearing in wrath.

Neither the love nor wrath of God are different from his essence. And therefore we may be sure that when [he] displays his love that it may be seen what the love of a God is. And also when he [displays his wrath it may be seen what the] wrath [of a God is.]

Both will be unspeakable.[1]

So preached Jonathan Edwards about heaven and hell. Both will be unspeakable because both reveal God in his ineffable essence—the one as love, the other as wrath.

In the pages that follow this truly awesome picture of the dual destiny of mankind will be filled out by the greatest biblical artist ever to draw it in such depth. Of one thing we are persuaded: what Edwards said, the Word of God said before him.

---

1. Exod. 9:12, "They that will not yield to the power of God's Word shall be broken by the power of his hand" (p. 2), July 1747, p. 31. Hereafter, as above, sermon texts will be followed by a "doctrine" and the page on which it occurs. All dates of manuscripts prior to 1733, at which time Edwards began to date them, are based on the careful calculations of Professor Thomas A. Schafer. If the sermon has been published in the two-volume Hickman edition of the *Works* (London, 1837) this is so noted. Occasionally other *Works* are cited. If the sermon was also preached elsewhere this, too, is entered in our note. Wherever possible we transcribe from the manuscript (unless the material was published in Edwards's own lifetime) with as few changes as possible, usually in spelling or the addition of essential punctuation.

We have quoted extensively and often at considerable length. This is not merely to provide the very language of the texts thereby avoiding any misinterpretation but also to capture some of the very spirit of the man which we often find lacking in works about him which by compression lose flavor if they do not introduce their own. Furthermore, many of these quotations are from unpublished manuscripts not easily available to the general reader and rarely cited in secondary works. The reader must realize that citing the manuscripts in their approximately pristine form is, in a sense, unfair to Edwards since he never had opportunity to prepare for, or even consent to, publication. This is the reason that some of the nineteenth-century editors tended to bowdlerize, but we consider our procedure the lesser of the two evils.

We take this occasion to express our profound gratitude to Miss Marjorie Wynne and the Beinecke Rare Book and Manuscript Library of Yale University for permission to use its Edwards collection and for unvarying, excellent library service.

Contents

1
Heaven

"When I think how great this happiness is sometimes it seems about incredible."

Someone has written of Edwards that he cared nothing for this world, spoke little of heaven, but certainly knew his hell. Edwards did know his hell, but he knew his heaven even better. Anyone who could say that he spoke little of heaven would surely have amused the people of Northampton who heard hundreds of sermons referring to this celestial theme, a number of them exclusively. If he spoke more of hell, it was only because he feared more people were going there, and he desired to set them on their way to heaven. If he spoke more of hell, it was supremely because the Bible speaks more of hell than of heaven.

In comparison with heaven, earth is insignificant; but its relation to heaven is utterly crucial. Our fleeting moments here determine where our eternity will be spent. "If men would go to heaven, they must first be made fit for it."[2]

To be made fit for heaven is to have one's heart in heaven. It has often been said that heaven is in the saint before the saint is in heaven. This is virtually the theme of the Matthew 6:21 and Isaiah 35:8 sermons. "Tis a thing of great consequence to men that their hearts should be in heaven."[3] Men's hearts being in heaven implies four things: that "their thoughts—their choices, their affections and their dependence is there."[4] This way of

2. Col. 1:12 (2), Stockbridge Indians, Aug. 1756, p. 1.
3. Matt. 6:21 (p. 2), May 1745.
4. *Ibid.*, p. 3.

communicating with God and Jesus is "sweet conversation within view of heaven."[5] This sweet conversation makes "the difficult duties of Christianity easy." Otherwise, the "way uphill" is hard.[6] Not only so, but "hearts not in heaven tis a sign they belong to hell."[7]

For Edwards, "those only that are holy are in the way to heaven."[8] Everyone, he preached, hopes to go to heaven but will not because holiness is "absolutely necessary." Otherwise, "if everyone that hoped for heaven ever got there, heaven by this time would have been full of murderers, adulterers, common swearers, drunkards, thieves, robbers and licentious debauchers."[9] No, he insists, holiness is absolutely necessary "in order to escape hell."[10] But holiness is not the morose, melancholy practice we are often led to think from childhood, but, on the contrary, "the amiable and excellent nature of it is enough to make it worthy the most earnest seeking after."[11] Holiness is "sweet," he concludes, "indeed ravishingly lovely."

It was appropriate that Edwards conclude his funeral sermon for David Brainerd exhorting the congregation that "in the way of such an holy life, we may at last come to so blessed an end."[12] The homily is a full description of what is commonly called today the "intermediate state." Many entries in Edwards's *Miscellanies*[13] deal with "separated saints"—the term with which he designated the intermediate state. Here five points are mentioned: first, the separated saints are in "the same blessed abode with the

---

5. *Ibid.*, p. 14.
6. *Ibid.*, p. 16.
7. *Ibid.*, p. 18.
8. Isa. 35:8, between fall 1722 and spring 1723, p. 4.
9. *Ibid.*, p. 4.
10. *Ibid.*, p. 15.
11. *Ibid.*, p. 16.
12. II Cor. 5:8, "The soul of a saint when it leaves the body at death goes to be with Christ" (p. 7). "Prepared for Mr. [David] Brainerd's funeral appointed Oct. 12, 1747." Hickman, II, 36f.
13. The *Miscellanies* are some 1,400 entries on various subjects recorded by Edwards from 1722 until the year of his death. These very important reflections range from a paragraph to a book. Many of them have been quite imperfectly edited and published. Mr. Schafer is presently working on a definitive edition of all of them for the Yale University Press edition of Edwards's *Works*. For our present volume the *Miscellanies* are used but not quite so much as the sermons. Though they are intellectually more basic than the sermons, we are slightly more concerned here with Edwards's message to the whole church and not merely to the scholars.

glorified human nature of Christ''; second, they have an "immediate view of Christ''; and third, a "most perfect conformity to" Christ; fourth, they enjoy "sweet converse with Christ''; and, fifth, a "glorious communion" with him as well.
For the saint, this world is but a pilgrimage to heaven. "This life ought so to be spent by us as to be only a journey towards heaven."[14] Consequently, "we ought not to rest in the world and its enjoyments, but should desire heaven." Temporal enjoyments only "serve a present turn." Our journey is "uphill" all the way, so we must "begin early"[15] and travel hard and long, every day, preparing for death. Growing in holiness is "coming nearer and nearer to heaven." And Christians should do this together, helping "one another up the hill." Twenty-two years later, as he was approaching the summit himself, Edwards was still saying the same thing to the Indians—it is an "uphill" climb to heaven.[16]

The Nature of Heaven

"... the eternal embraces and the eternal joys. ..."

Heaven is the place of unmixed and unending happiness as incapable of exaggeration as are the miseries of the damned. "There is scarce any thing that can be conceived or expressed about the degree of the happiness of the saints in heaven. ..."[17] The intimacy is based on the incarnation, which admits man "to the inmost fellowship with the Deity." "It seems," Edwards continues, "to be God's design to admit the church into the divine family as his Son's wife." The atonement is the supreme bond of intimacy for "Christ will surely give himself as much to his saints as he has given himself for them. He whose arms were opened to suffer to be nailed to the cross will doubtless be opened as wide to embrace those for whom he suffered."

---

14. Heb. 11:13, 14. Cf. note on p. 2.

15. *Ibid.*, pp. 2-13.

16. Cf. Rev. 22:5, "The saints in heaven shall have light without any darkness" (p. 1), St. Aug., 1756, p. 4.

17. M741. This is the way I shall designate *Miscellanies* in this volume.

Edwards had laid the foundation for a definition of heaven in one of his earliest *Miscellanies* written when he was about twenty years of age: "'. . . contrary to the opinion of Hobbes (that nothing is substantial but matter) no matter is substance but only God who is a spirit.'' Other spirits also are substantial but matter is no substance at all.[18] Consequently it followed in all his preaching that heaven, where the saints "enjoy God as their portion,'' is the place of real, substantial happiness.[19]

Sometimes heaven seems supersubstantial:

> Thus they shall eat and drink abundantly, and swim in the ocean of love, and be eternally swallowed up in the infinitely bright, and infinitely mild and sweet, beams of divine love; eternally receiving that light, eternally full of it, and eternally compassed round with it, and everlastingly reflecting it back again to its fountain.[20]

This is a description of Brainerd's present heaven.

Basing an address on the fact that the Revelation metaphor of "transparent gold'' speaks of something beyond reality or imagination Edwards nevertheless gives us eight figures of this truth before pointing out the insufficiency of all of them and then lines up seven arguments from reason and seven more from Scripture for the truth of this transcendental. Whereupon he considers four respects in which this truth is unknown and ends with an extensive and searching application. We will settle for the doctrine taken from Revelation 21:18, "There is nothing upon earth that will suffice to represent to us the glory of heaven.''[21]

Interestingly, teenage Edwards had written in his very first extant sermon, that on Isaiah 3:10:

> to pretend to describe the excellence, the greatness or duration of the happiness of heaven by the most artful composition of words would be but to darken and cloud it, to talk of raptures and ecstacies, joy and singing, is but to set forth very low shadows of

---

18. Mf. The *Miscellanies* were first designated by letters and then double letters until Edwards went over to numerals up to 1,360.

19. M1072.

20. II Cor. 5:8. Hickman, II, 29. Cf. also Rom. 2:10, "The portion of the righteous.'' Cf. also Mf.

21. Rev. 21:18 (1) and (2), between fall of 1723 and winter 1726, p. 4. M508 observes that heaven is better than the original Paradise.

the reality, and all we can say by our best rhetoric is really and truly, vastly below what is but the bare and naked truth, and if St. Paul who had seen them, thought it but in vain to endeavor to utter it much less shall we pretend to do it, and the Scriptures have gone as high in the descriptions of it as we are able to keep pace with it in our imaginations and conception. . . .[22]

The Lord's Supper here below is a foretaste of the ineffably sublime heavenly communion.[23]

Much of the perfect happiness of heaven is the fellowship of the saints there. It is sweet here but perfect there; anticipation here, fulfillment there. "They shall have great delight in the society and enjoyment of one another. . . . The saints in heaven shall all be one society, they shall be united together without any schism, there shall be sweet harmony, and a perfect union."[24]

A special pleasure ("peculiar comfort") of the communion of saints in heaven is that they will recognize their former Christian friends from earth. It is true that in our present condition natural affection is a duty, and the absence of it is the sign of a very vicious disposition, "but this is no virtue in the saints in glory."[25] Nevertheless, "there is no reason to think, that the friendships contracted here on earth between saints that have been sanctified by the love of God will be rooted out in another world."[26] So, saints will recognize fellow saints in heaven and the love for them will be perfected. *future tense*.

This is wonderful for friends. But what about enemies? Disputes also will be settled at the day of judgment as some parties are vindicated and rewarded with heaven while others are condemned and punished. This was the poignant anticipation which Edwards expressed to his Northampton congregation in the "Farewell Sermon" after the grueling controversy that dissolved the pastoral relationship.

---

22. Isa. 3:10, "A good man is a happy man whatever his outward condition is," before fall of 1722, p. 8.
23. Luke 22:20, "The saints shall hereafter as it were eat and drink with Christ at his table in his Kingdom of Glory" (p. 4).
24. Rom. 2:10, "Glory, honor, and peace is the portion that God has given to all the godly" (p. 2), Dec. (probably) 1735, p. 67.
25. Rev. 18:20, p. 20.
26. Rom. 2:10, pp. 72, 73.

How highly therefore does it now become us, to consider of that time when we must meet one another before the chief Shepherd! When I must give an account of my stewardship, of the service I have done, and the reception and treatment I have had among the people to whom he sent me. And you will give an account of your own conduct towards me, and the improvement you have made of these three and twenty years of my ministry. For then both you and I must appear together, and we both must give an account, in order to an infallible, righteous and eternal sentence to be passed upon us, by him who will judge us with respect to all that we have said or done in our meetings here. . . . There is nothing covered, that shall not be revealed, nor hid, which shall not be known; all will be examined in the searching, penetrating light of God's omniscience and glory . . . our hearts will be turned inside out. . . .[27]

Then "he will declare what is right between them, approving him that has been just and faithful, and condemning the unjust; and perfect truth and equity shall take place in the sentence which he passes, in the rewards he bestows, and the punishments which he inflicts."[28]

The very episode in Northampton is characteristic of the present world. There is no perfect happiness here. One person flourishes while another is cast down and then the reverse follows. These vicissitudes are meant to prepare us for heaven where we will experience unfluctuating joy.[29]

But permanent happiness does come in heaven because God is there. However joyous the company of the redeemed, friends, old and new, the real life of the heavenly party is God himself. The love of Christian family and friends are but the drops; God is the ocean.[30] "They shall enter into the king's palace."[31]

It is especially by union with Christ that this perfect enjoyment

27. II Cor. 1:14, "Ministers, and the people that have been under their care, must meet one another before Christ's tribunal at the day of judgment." "Farewell Sermon" delivered July 1, 1750. Hickman, I, ccxlvi.

28. *Ibid.*, p. ccxliv.

29. M585.

30. Cf. II Cor. 5:1, "The saints when their present state in this world is ended will go to heaven. . . ." (p. 1), May 1747.

31. Ps. 45:15. Lecture, March 1744. This is a long outline lecture making five points. Heaven is first defined as God's palace. Then it is described along with the character of those who enter it as well as the manner of their entrance. Finally comes the crucial point: in what quality and to what purpose they enter.

which makes heaven heaven comes about. The saints possess "all things," but this is in Jesus Christ. Edwards explained this in detail in an early *Miscellany*.

> Union with Christ. By virtue of the believer's union with Christ, he doth really possess all things.... I'll tell you what I mean by possessing all things. I mean that God, three in one, all that he is, and all that he has, and all that he does, all that he has made or done, the whole universe, bodies and spirits, light, heaven, angels, men and devils, sun, moon, stars, land, sea, fish and fowls, all the silver and gold, kings and potentates, as well as mere men, are as much the Christian's as the money in his pocket, the clothes he wears, or the house he dwells in, as the victuals he eats; yea, more properly his, more advantageously, more his than if he commands all those things mentioned to be just in all respects as he pleased, at any time, by virtue of the union with Christ, because Christ who certainly doth thus possess all things is entirely his, so that he possesses it all.... only he has not the trouble of managing of it but Christ to whom it is no trouble, manages it for him, a thousand times as much to his advantage as he could himself, if he had the managing of all.... And who would desire to possess all things more than to have all things managed just according to his will....

Is it any wonder that at times Edwards finds heaven itself almost too good to be true? But he argues himself down.[32] This matter is spelled out in fulness by showing that the denial of the perfection of heaven is an implicit denial of the perfection of the work of Christ.[33] In other words, if Christ is true, heaven must be true also. There is, to be sure, an infinite distance between God and the saints, but the blood of Christ, the God-man, removes all such hindrances to intimacy. The distance between the two natures—divine and human—is overcome by the one who combines both in his one person.

Consequently, the saints are emboldened to go directly to Christ and to God and far more than they would ever freely approach angels or intercessors. It is Christ who unites men and angels to each other. One could say, in the spirit of Edwards, that Christ is our intercessor with men (including Mary) and angels, rather than the other way around. He ends this lengthy theological

---

32. M741.
33. *Ibid.*

discussion by depicting the intimacy of Christ and the saints in terms of the Song of Songs. Christ took human nature for the purpose of being closer to men. This closeness is realized fully only in heaven.[34]

(In fact, it is because of Christ's work of redemption that men are brought nearer to God than the angels are. The latter have only their own righteousness while Christians possess the righteousness of Christ.[35] In a late *Miscellany* Edwards gives one of his most exquisite descriptions of heaven in terms of Jesus Christ:[36]

> The external heaven surrounds Christ not merely as an house surrounds an inhabitant or as a palace surrounds a prince or as stones and timber encompass a land. But rather as plants and flowers are before the sun that have their life and beauty and being from that luminary or as the sun may be encompassed round with reflections of his brightness as the cloud of glory in Mt. Sinai surrounded Christ there.

All of this, wonderful as it sounds, is but the wedding rehearsal. The grand event of heaven, which goes on forever, is the wedding feast of Christ and his bride, the church, where we will enjoy "the eternal embraces and the eternal joys."[37]

⌒ The Locality of Heaven

"... part of the universe ... the highest or outermost part of it ..."

As we have seen, heaven is a state of incredible happiness. Is it also a state like Michigan or Pennsylvania? There can be no doubt that, for Jonathan Edwards, the state of bliss is also a place in space (too far out for the astronauts). This is the place to which the soul of the penitent thief went—"Paradise."[38] There could be

---

34. M957.
35. Deut. 30:19, "I. The benefit that is to be obtained by righteousness is life....," St. Ind., May 1755.
36. M1122.
37. M957.
38. II Cor. 5:8. Hickman, II, 27.

some question of the locality of heaven during the intermediate
state but hardly in the post-resurrection period. One doctrine that
makes it immediately evident that heaven is in some particular
locality is the resurrection of the body. Bodies occupy space and
can be in but one place at a time. Of course, Edwards had no
doubt about the resurrection of the bodies of the saints nor the
place to which they go—heaven.

> The dead in Christ shall arise at the sound of the last trumpet with
> glo[rified] bodies, and the living saints shall see them. The holy
> and blessed souls of saints that descended from heaven with
> Christ, shall then be brought to their bodies to be reunited to them
> that shall be prepared by infinite wisdom and skill to be fit organs
> for a holy and happy soul. . . .[39]

Although heaven is the place where gloriously visible saints
go, it is essentially the place where God's glorious manifestation
abides. "Heaven is everywhere in Scripture represented as the
throne of God, and that part of the universe, that is God's fixed
abode, and dwelling-place, and that is everlastingly appropriated
to that use."[40] There are many places where God has manifested
himself from time to time, but his fixed abode of manifestation is
called heaven, and it remains.[41]

What about the "new heavens"? What Scripture calls the
"new heavens and the new earth" is a reference to the renovation
of the world here below. Heaven above never changes. The
heaven of God is not a temple made with hands.

> Heaven is the place whence Christ descended, and it is the place
> whither he ascended. It was the place whence the Holy Ghost
> descended on Christ, and whence the voice came, saying, This is
> my beloved Son, in whom I am well pleased; and is the place
> whence the Holy Ghost was poured out at Pentecost: and whatever
> is from God is said to be from heaven. . . .[42]

Another argument which is offered against this renovated
world being heaven is earth's mobility. It is now constantly in

39. Rom. 2:10, p. 44.
40. M743. Hickman, II, 630.
41. *Ibid.*, 630, 631.
42. *Ibid.*, 631.

motion and would seem to have to continue to be so if its nature were not fundamentally altered. That is beneath the dignity of the throne of God; not to mention the fact that heaven is said to be unshakable and God's kingdom one that cannot be moved.[43]

Nevertheless, heaven permanently fixed as it is, is capable of further glory. Explaining this, Edwards is at his mystical and hermeneutical best. Just as the body of Christ was glorified and his human soul as well, it is fitting that the outer dwelling of God should undergo a change for the better:

> The external heavens, and the human nature of Christ, are the *external house* and *temple* of God in different senses; but the human nature, or body, of Christ, including both the head and the members,—including his human nature with his church,—is the house and temple of God in the highest sense. This is immensely the most noble temple of God. But if this, which is the palace of God in so much the highest sense, will pass under a glorious change; why should not the external house, which is the temple of God in a much inferior sense, and which indeed is to be but a house for this house, pass under a glorious change? If the inner temple, the highest and most holy part of the temple, shall be so much exalted, why may we not suppose that the external temple . . . be changed and made proportionally more beautiful. . . . If the soul shall be glorified and made better, why not the body? if the body, why not the garment? if the inhabitants, why not the house?[44]

Later, Edwards raises the question whether this glorification of the highest heaven will be done by the Father or the Son. He gives a seven-point answer that this must be the work of the Son when he brings his bride to her new and everlasting dwelling.[45]

That heaven is a glorious and fixed location Edwards feels certain, and its location is the third or outermost heaven. But, what is the significance of it and particularly of Paul's ascending there? In answer to that question Edwards gives a superb explanation in a note in his *Blank Bible*[46] which we must quote in full:

> When the Old Testament saints and prophets have been admitted to so great a privilege, tis not unreasonable to suppose that

---

43. *Ibid.*, 631f.
44. *Ibid.*, 634.
45. *Ibid.*, 636, 637.
46. The *Blank Bible* is an interleaved one in which Edwards made annotations.

New Testament saints and apostles should be admitted to as great and greater of the like kind, considering how much more glorious the dispensation is that the latter are ministers of than the other, and how much more honourable the minister. John the Baptist that was only the forerunner of Christ was greater than the greatest of the Old Testament prophets, and Christ tells us the least in the Kingdom of Heaven is greater than he. But Paul was the greatest minister in the Kingdom of Heaven. The glory of the dispensation that Moses was minister of and that shining of his face was a signification of, was no glory in comparison of the glory of that dispensation that Paul was minister of as he himself particularly declares in the third chapter of this epistle magnifying his office. Paul was the principal minister of the New Testament as Moses was the principal minister of the Old. Paul was the great apostle of the Gentiles and revealer of the gospel to them and founder of the Gentile Church as Moses was the greatest prophet of the Jews and revealer of the law to them and founder of the Jewish Church. It is probable that when Paul ascended into heaven that he there received his gospel that he preached to the Gentiles that he so often speaks of, of Jesus Christ, and it was suitable there should be such a difference that Paul should receive his Gospel in heaven as Moses did the law on Mount Sinai—that that dispensation which was earthly and contained only an image of the heavenly should be communicated on earth only on a mountain where was an image of heaven, but that the heavenly things themselves should be communicated in heaven itself. As the glory of Moses's dispensation was no glory in comparison of Paul's so the glory of Mount Sinai was no glory in comparison of the glory of the third heaven.[47]

The Degrees of Blessedness

"The saints are like so many vessels of different sizes cast into a sea of happiness where every vessel is full."

There is first, second, and third class in heaven as well as on earth and in hell. The published sermon on John 14:2, "Many Mansions"[48] describes the different accommodations and their

---

47. *Blank Bible* note on II Cor. 12:2-4, pp. 834, 835.
48. John 14:2 (2), "I. That heaven is God's house, and II. that in this house of God there are many mansions" (p. 3). The sabbath after the seating the new meeting house, Dec. 25, 1737. N. Gardiner, *Selected Sermons*, 1904.

respective costs. To change the metaphor drastically: saints are vessels all filled with joy but differing in size.[49] All receive a crown but of different luster.[50] Again, they are all in the mystical body of Christ in various positions. "He makes whom he pleases the feet and whom he pleases the hand and whom he pleases the lungs, etc."[51]

Before we raise the question whether the differing prestige among saints could "raise hell" in heaven, as it did on earth, as it did in the Garden, and before that in the original heaven, we must first find out how an uncompromising solafidean such as Paul made room for "rewards" in the first place. If all is of grace and there is no merit whatsoever in believers, how can there be status symbols in a Christian heaven? Is this a return to Roman Catholicism? Has Edwards forgotten all about mere grace and introduced sheer works?

Needless to say, Edwards would not sell himself out consciously. He is fully aware of the appearances and is quite ready to prove that these appearances are deceiving. Not only does he call these "free" rewards, but he spells the whole matter out with evangelical thoroughness. "However mean and polluted what the saints do is in itself," he asserts, "yet all the pollution that attends it is hid, and everything they do for God that has the least sincerety in it is precious in God's eyes, through his infinite grace, and shall in no case lose its reward, neither shall it in any wise lose its honour at the day of judgment. They shall receive praise and glory in reward for it."[52]

If this sounds like teacher's-petism, as if God were blind to the faults of "saints" and able to see only their infinitesimal virtues while proceeding quite in the reverse manner with the "sinners," the reader must remember the Edwardsean salvific context. When men fell they became sinners only and always until the elect (their guilt being expiated by Christ), were converted and justified by him. Subsequently, all their remaining "pollution" is "hid"

49. M367 and Titus 3:5, "That there are none saved by their own righteousness" (p. 3), n.d.

50. James 1:12 (1), "... that those who love Christ shall receive of him a crown of life." Between fall 1722 and spring 1723. This is the second part of the sermon on James 1:12, the first part having been delivered in the "forenoon."

51. M403.

52. Rom. 2:10, p. 49.

from God only in the sense that he sees it as expiated guilt. Meanwhile the true virtue which springs from their redeemed and regenerated souls, indwelt by the Holy Spirit, is accepted as having the root of virtue as it does. Thus God is dealing justly with the saints and not unjustly with the sinners.

Nevertheless, we may ask, will it not be extremely embarrassing for the saints at the day of judgment? No, because, "if the sins of the saints shall be rehearsed, it shall not be for their shame, but for the glory of divine grace; to give opportunity for them to plead the atonement of the Saviour who will be the Judge, to give occasion to them to produce Christ's righteousness, which will surely be accepted by himself."[53]

Imperfect "good works" are not only accepted in Christ but they are the rule according to which "free rewards" are given. They are not the basis of rewards (only Christ is that, and, furthermore, even perfect human works would not deserve any reward)[54] but they are the rule according to which unmerited rewards are distributed. Augustine inferred this, but it took Edwards to explicate it. "Rewards of grace" or "free rewards" articulate both concepts—grace and reward. "Grace" Edwards honors by insisting that the rewards are pure gifts utterly unearned and "rewards" he honors by showing that these unearned gifts are distributed according to a rule or proportion of works, thus putting body into the term *reward* without sacrificing its gracious character.[55]

Edwards carefully accounts for the rewards of saints saved by grace. First, he clears the apparent inconsistency between the pure grace of God and a role for the works of saints. Christ, he argued, purchased perfect happiness but this did not prevent differing degrees of it.

> The saints are like so many vessels of different sizes cast into a sea of happiness where every vessel is full: this is eternal life, for a man ever to have his capacity filled. But after all tis left to God's sovereign pleasure, tis his prerogative to determine the largeness

---

53. *Ibid.*, pp. 50, 51.

54. Luke 17:9, "That God don't thank men for doing those things which he commands them" (p. 2), fall 1727.

55. I Peter 2:5, "The good works of the godly can't be accepted any other way than in and through Christ" (p. 5), before 1733.

of the vessel.... Christ's death and righteousness meddled not
with this but left it in God's prerogative....[56]

The covenant of works would not have "meddled with it" either.
"If Adam's perfect obedience would not have been concerned in
it, then Christ's perfect obedience..."[57] would not either. The
bottom line is that Christ's obedience only merited perfect
happiness—no more, no less. The saints can claim no "rewards"
from Christ's work. Even Christ himself is subject to the sovereignty of God in the matter of rewards.

As one would anticipate, Edwards would not let matters rest at
this point but sooner or later would attempt to define "capacity"
in the saints. This concept he discusses in M817.[58] Here he finds
four factors that determine degrees of reward: 1. "degrees of
grace and holiness here" (in this world); 2. "degree of the good
that is done"; 3. "self-denial and suffering"; and 4. "eminency
in humility."[59]

Thus it becomes clear that the degree of glory will not be
precisely equal to the degree of grace in this world. Edwards later
adds something to capacity by including the "enjoying faculty"
or openness to receive grace. He then lists three qualities of this
faculty:[60] extent and strength; knowledge; and degree and manner
of the views. These cravings which are now frustrated will then
be filled.

But does this not make heaven the reward of self-seekers? The
desire for rewards is based, Edwards acknowledges, on the principle of self-love. Self-love, however, is in itself a good, or, at
least, neutral principle.[61] Only inordinate self-concern is a sin.
Even Christ prayed for his own happiness, according to John
17:5. It will be our love of God which will influence us to do the
good works for which we know we must be rewarded.[62]

---

56. M367.
57. *Ibid.* In a footnote Edwards reminds himself "where I have used such expressions
as that Christ purchased that every man's capacity should be filled, to put instead thereof
this: that Christ purchased 'complete and perfect happiness according to his capacity'
because tis uncertain in what sense glorified saints' capacity may be said to be filled."
58. Cf. also M822.
59. M817.
60. M822.
61. *The Nature of True Virtue,* Hickman, I, 122f.
62. II Cor. 9:6, "We ought to seek high degrees of glory in heaven" (p. 5), Feb.
1736–37.

So Edwards revels in appeals to abound in reward-winning good works. "We ought to seek high degrees of glory in heaven."[63] Nothing could be gained by good works if there were no reward, and it seems preposterous that nothing could be gained by good works. In fact, we ministers do not have to apologize for the appeal to rewards but may use them freely. These appetites for reward cannot be overindulged. "Persons need not and ought not to set any bounds to their spiritual and gracious appetites."[64] Do not, he pleads, sow sparingly. Seek the most ample rooms in the heavenly kingdom. An aristocrat in all his ways, Edwards intended to go first class in heaven and urged his people to do so as well.

The sky is literally the limit. All degrees notwithstanding it is well to recall that, for Edwards, in the very last analysis, there is "scarce anything that can be conceived or expressed about the degree of happiness of the saints in heaven."[65] The blood of Christ removes all hindrance to joy.

Growth in Blessedness

"The most perfect rest is consistent with being continually employed."

If there are differing degrees of glory among heaven's inhabitants, there are also different stages in heaven by which they reach their zenith in glory. But before that, comes the preparation for heaven in this world.

"The saints growing ripe for heaven" is the theme of the Revelation 14:15 sermon.[66] Edwards finds four elements involved in the greening of the saints. First, he notes that "grace at its first infusion into the soul is usually very imperfect."[67] "Our vines have tender grapes,"[68] and these tender grapes are not so

---

63. *Ibid.*
64. Cant. 5:1 (p. 3), between summer and fall, 1729.
65. M741.
66. Jan. 1743–44, p. 4.
67. *Ibid.*
68. Cant. 2:15.

sweet nor as useful as they are to become. Saints in this world are, second, in a preparatory state;[69] third, in a progressive state,[70] and, most important, becoming "more and more fit for their heavenly state."[71] "The saints in the progress they make in grace and holiness are brought more and more to an actual preparedness forever to leave this world."[72] Referring especially to young people or new converts the preacher astutely observes, alluding to "much false zeal,"[73] that "many kinds of fruit while they are green have a great deal of bitterness and sourness, are very sweet when they are fully ripe and fit to be gathered."[74] He concludes with this image or shadow of divine things: "The sweetness of ripe fruit is a fit emblem of the holy sweetness of his disposition that is ripe for heaven."[75] A fifth evidence of ripening is purity without mixture.[76] Solidity of the fruit is the sixth evidence,[77] and finally,[78] surprisingly, is assurance, because "in order to an actual fitness for heaven a person should know that he belongs there."

While the proper time for rewards is not until the end of the world, the saints will "have glorious rewards in heaven immediately after death."[79] But after that the rewards continue in the form of ever-new discoveries of one another, in contrast to this life. "How soon do earthly lovers come to an end of their discoveries of each other's beauty; how soon do they see all that is to be seen!"[80] But in heaven there is "eternal progress" with new beauties always being discovered.

The resurrection is a period of special growth in heavenly felicity.[81] It will exceed the saints' present state of glory, just as the gospel state excels the Mosaic dispensation. When saints now go to glory they see Christ directly. Being absent from the body

69. Rev. 14:15, p. 6.
70. *Ibid.*, p. 8.
71. *Ibid.*, p. 13.
72. *Ibid.*, p. 15.
73. *Ibid.*, p. 30.
74. *Ibid.*, p. 31.
75. *Ibid.*, p. 33.
76. *Ibid.*
77. *Ibid.*, p. 36.
78. *Ibid.*, p. 37.
79. M775.
80. M198.
81. M710.

they are present with the Lord. Nevertheless, though there is no darkness there, because sin is gone, the glory is "dim." Edwards compares this heavenly state before the resurrection of the body to the quiet before the wedding. "The saints now in heaven see God or the divine nature by a reflex light comparatively with the manner in which they will see it after the resurrection; seeing now through the glass of the glorified human nature of Christ and in the glass of his works especially relating to redemption...."[82] Many refinements of growth in "bodily" pleasures take place at the resurrection. The saints will then have "refined bodies" which put minds in a "sprightly frame." Minds in turn, "shall cause a sweet sensation throughout the body, infinitely excelling any sensual pleasure here."[83] They will continue to see and hear but the medium "will be infinitely finer" and more receptive. "So the eye may be so much more sensible and the medium, the rays, so much more exquisite that for aught we know they may distinctly see the beauty of one another's countenances and smiles, and hold a delightful and most intimate conversation at a thousand miles distance."[84] Their bodies will be more effulgent than the sun. Indeed it will be a different (Rev. 21:11), and finer light than the sun,[85] with new and more wonderful colors. Every faculty will be "an inlet of delight."

Eternality and fixity of a state usually suggest the absence of any possible growth. Growth means change which seems to preclude fixity. Difference from time to time appears inconsistent with a thing's being eternal. But there is both change and growth in heaven since the growth is only within. The state of eternal blessedness is one in which there is no change ever—for that activity is in rest. Though they enjoy perfect rest, yet they are a great deal more active than they were when in this world. After

---

82. *Ibid.* In this connection Edwards notes in a corollary that the angels were created for this grand consummation when God communicates himself to the human creature. They were created in the first place to witness the creation of this world and this is the grand consummation of that creation. On the other hand, the angels were condemned who used the Lord's people for merchandise as were ministers who "lorded it over" them. The classic example is the Roman Catholic church of which Egypt is the type in Rev. 11:8. For the saints, "all things are yours"; good angels and bad minister to your ultimate resurrection glory.
83. M233.
84. M263.
85. M721. Cf. also M95, M188, M893, M957.

describing how the saints will be brought to their "last perfection"[86] in heaven after the day of judgment, Edwards hastily
adds, "not that I determine that there will be no gradual increase
of happiness in the saints and angels after."[87]

How did he know, however desirable it may be to contemplate,
that the saints will be active and growing eternally? We find
several reasons scattered throughout his writings and preach-
ments. First, man is rational and must, to be happy, be rationally
active. Second, the saints will see the damned and ever increas-
ingly appreciate their own good fortune. Third, the remembrance
of their own sins will cause them to grow in their gratitude.
Fourth, the knowledge of the unfolding of the work of redemption has the same effect.

The reason that heaven means rest from trouble and not toil is
that perfection of happiness does not consist in idleness, but on
the contrary, it very much consists in action. To the Indians
Edwards stated it cryptically: "rest and ease without labour."[88]
The happiness of rational creatures very much consists in action.[89] "The most perfect rest is consistent with being continually
employed."[90] Six ways in which the joy of heaven is partly in the
active serving of God are pointed out.[91] Elsewhere he observes:
"In heaven 'tis the directly reverse of what 'tis on earth; for
there, by length of time things become more and more youthful,
that is, more vigorous, active, tender, and beautiful."[92]

Edwards is naturally quite concerned about intellectual activity
in heaven and devotes a number of *Miscellanies* to pursuing this
interest. Possibly no one in history devoted more intellectual
energy in this world contemplating intellectual activity in the
world to come. We can anticipate here that the beatific vision is
going to be the *amor intellectualis Dei*. But returning to the lesser

---

86. Jude 6, "The day of judgment will be a great day," May 1744, Jan. 1754, Feb.
1758, St. Ind., p. 13.

87. *Ibid.*

88. Rev. 22:5, "The saints in heaven shall have light without any darkness," St. Aug.,
1756, p. 1.

89. Rev. 22:3, "That the happiness of the saints in heaven consists partly in that they
there serve God" (p. 2), March 13, 1731.

90. Rev. 14:2, "The work of saints in heaven doth very much consist in praising
God," Nov. 7, 1734. Dwight, VIII, 305f.

91. *Ibid.*

92. M206.

perfections of heaven for the moment, we are told that "I argue from this foundation, that their [the saints'] number of ideas shall increase to eternity.'"[93] They will, from the very beginning, remember this world and the growth of the church and go on remembering for millions of millions of ages. If there were only one idea in such vast periods, even that would spell infinite growth. So the saints will increase in knowledge (and holiness) to eternity.

Edwards stops to face the objection that according to this reasoning the damned would grow in perfection also since they too would be learning more. True, they will be learning more, but they only grow in odiousness as they increase in knowledge because of their incorrigible disposition, allowing knowledge only to puff up. "The more knowing, *caeteris paribus,* capable of more [wickedness].'"[94] We will pursue this further in our discussion of hell.

Second, although the wicked in hell will improve their knowledge to more odiousness, heaven's contemplation of those in hell will be only a further increase in wholesome knowledge.

'Tis the nature of pleasure and pain of happiness and misery that they greatly quicken and heighten the sense of each other. . . . The saints in glory therefore when they shall see the doleful state that the damned are in, how will this heighten their sense of the blessedness of their own state, that is so exceeding different from it.[95]

Third, the remembrance of their own sins will cause them to grow in appreciation of grace. Even though the righteous in heaven can contemplate hell and thereby increase in edifying knowledge, one wonders whether the remembrance of their own sins and folly in this world may not cast a shadow of gloom over their perfect happiness. No, explains Edwards, for though they will see

a thousand times as much of the evil and folly of sin as they do now; yet they will not experience any proper sorrow or grief for it, for this reason, because they will so perfectly see at the same

93. M105.
94. *Ibid.*
95. Rev. 18:20, pp. 15, 16.

time, how that 'tis turned to the best to the glory of God . . . and
particularly they will have so much the more admiring and joyful
sense of God's grace in pardoning them, that the remembrance of
their sins will rather be an indirect occasion of joy.[96]

Returning to the direct consideration of the increase in knowledge we find Edwards exulting in the anticipation of being able to
intuit what is not possible now.

'Tis only for want of sufficient accurateness, strength, and comprehension of mind that from the motion of one particular atom
we can't tell [all] that ever has been that now is in the whole extent
of the creation, as to quantity of matter figure bulk and motion,
distance and every thing that ever shall be. Coroll. What room for
improvement of reason is there for angels and glorified minds![97]

The fullest and most penetrating reflection on this point is
found in M777:

Happiness of heaven is progressive and has various periods in
which it has a new and glorious advancement and consists very
much in *beholding* the manifestations that God makes of himself
in the *work of redemption.* There can be no view or knowledge
that one spiritual being can have of another, but it must be either
immediate and intuitive or mediate or some manifestations or
signs. An immediate and intuitive view of any mind, if it be
consequent and dependent on the prior existence of what is
viewed in that mind, is the very same with consciousness, for to
have an immediate view of a mind is to have an immediate view
of the thoughts, volitions, exercises, and motions of that mind, for
there is nothing else in any mind to be beheld, but to have an
immediate view of the idea and exercises of any mind consequent
on their existence is the same as to have an immediate perception,
sense, or feeling of them as they pass or exist in that mind. For
there is no difference between immediate seeing ideas and immediate having them; neither is there any difference between a
created mind's immediate view of the sense or feelings of a mind
either of pleasure or pain and feeling the same; therefore a
spiritual created being can't have an immediate view of another
mind without some union of personality. If two spirits were so
made of God that the one evermore necessarily saw all that passed

96. M432.
97. M272.

in the other's mind fully and perceived it as in that mind so that all
the ideas & all the sense of things that was in one was fully viewed
by the other, or a full idea of all was necessarily constantly excited
in the one consequent on its being in the other and beheld as in the
other those two would to all intents & purposes be the same
individual person, & if it were not constantly but only for a season
there would be for a season an union of personality, and if those
seasons were determined by the will of one of them, viz. of him
whose ideas were consequent on those of the other when he
pleased to turn the attention of his mind to the other, still the effect
is the same—there is for a season an union of personality. If the
ideas and sense that pass in one, tho immediately perceived, yet
are not fully perceived but only in some degree, still this dont
hinder the effects being the same, viz. an union of personality in
some degree.

Therefore there is no creature can thus have an immediate sight
of God but only Jesus Christ who is in the bosom of God. For no
creature can have such an immediate view of another created
spirit, for if they could they could search the heart and try the
reins, but to see and *search the heart* is often spoken of as *God's
prerogative,* and as one thing God's divinity and infinite exalta-
tion above all creatures appears and God who is called the invisible God, Colos. 1.15; and the King eternal, immortal, invisible, 1 Tim 1.17; and he that is invisible, Heb. 11.27; and of
whom it is said 1 John 4.12, "No man (in the original no one)
hath seen God at any time," and 1 Tim. 6.16 who only hath
immortality dwelling in the light which no man can approach unto
whom no man (or no one) hath seen or can see. I say this being is
doubtless as invisible as created spirits & 'tis not to be thought
that gives no mere creature to an immediate sight or knowledge of
any created spirit but reserves it to himself and his Son as their
great prerogative properly belonging to them as God would admit
'em to an immediate sight or knowledge of himself whom to know
is an infinitely higher prerogative of the only begotten Son of
God, who is in the bosom of the Father.

Jesus Christ is admitted to know God immediately but the
knowledge of all other creatures in heaven & earth is by means or
by manifestations or signs held forth and Jesus Christ who alone
sees immediately, the grand medium of the knowledge of all
others they know no otherwise than by the exhibitions held forth
in any by him as the Scripture is express, Matt. 11.27. No man (in
the Hebrew, no one) knoweth the Son but the Father neither
knoweth any one the Father save the Son and he to whomsoever
the Son will reveal him and John 1.18, No one hath seen God at
any time, the only begotten Son which is in the bosom of the
Father he hath declared him, John 6.46. Not that any one hath

seen the Father save he which is of God, he hath seen the
Father. . . .

Fourth, the knowledge of the unfolding work of redemption
increases the saints' growth in happiness—just as it did in this
world. "It seems to be quite a wrong notion of the happiness of
heaven that . . . it admits not of new joys upon new occasions. . . .
It seems to me evident that the church in heaven have received
new joys from time to time upon new occasions. . . . The coming
of Christ I believe made an exceeding great addition. . . ."[98] And
so Edwards continues listing the raising of bodies when Christ
rose, Christ's own session in heaven, and the successes of the
gospel after the ascension.[99] He concludes, maintaining "that
their joy is increasing and will be increasing as God gradually in
his providence unveils his glory till the last day."[100] Of course,
not only at these major events in the history of redemption does
heaven itself advance but at the conversion of each sinner also.[101]

Finally, when Christ submits his kingdom to the Father there
will be a climactic implement of glory. God will then manifest his
favor to his Son, the bridegroom, and the church, his bride, and
the "eternal wedding"[102] will begin. Edwards is uncertain
whether there will be a greater glorification at that time of the
human or the divine nature of Christ as he pursues the discussion
of this fine point of ecstasy for several pages.

Heaven Beholding This World

*"The happiness of the saints in heaven consists much in behold-
ing the church on earth."*

Edwards does much reflecting on heaven's contemplating this
world. He is speaking above about heaven as it now is, not as it
will be in its consummate state after the resurrection. In fact, he

---

98. M372.
99. *Ibid.*
100. *Ibid.*
101. *Ibid.*
102. M957.

has a great deal to say about the "separate state" as, for example, in M555 and 565.[103] We will confine ourselves here to what he says about these "separated saints" in heaven as they observe the goings-on in our world. We must admit that this contemplation threatens the bliss of heaven, for it would seem, at first glance, that there is not too much in this world to make the saints in glory happy. If anything, there is much to disturb their peace. How wrong we are. Says Edwards, "The happiness of the saints in heaven consists much in beholding the displays of God's mercy towards his church on earth. . . ."[104] Even the saints here have an eye on God's activities. We should have immediately realized that the saints in glory would have an eye only for that. But how does Edwards know this? He argues it from the "meek shall inherit the earth" and

their having in the present time [in heaven, that is] much more given of this world, houses and lands, etc., than they parted with in the suffering state of the church; from Christ's comforting his disciples, when about to leave them, that they should weep and lament, and the world rejoice, yet their sorrow should be turned into joy, as a woman has sorrow in her travail, but much more than joy enough to balance it when she is delivered; from its being promised to the good man, Ps. cxxviii., that he should see the prosperity of Jerusalem, and peace in Israel; from the manner in which the promises of the future prosperity of the church were made of old to the church then in being; and from the manner in which the saints received them as all their salvation, and all their desire, and are said to hope and await for the fulfillment from time to time.[105]

A couple *Miscellanies* later, we find David taking great consolation in the fact that God promised that he would see his kingdom established. All these considerations lead Edwards to the grand conclusion that "the blessedness of the church triumphant in heaven, and their joy and glory, will as much consist in beholding the success of Christ's redemption on earth, and in as great proportion, as the joy that was set before Christ consists in it, or

---

103. Hickman, II, 622f.
104. M1059. Hickman, II, 637.
105. Hickman, II, 637.

as the glory and reward of Christ as God-man and Mediator consists in it.''[106]

A number of Edwards's latest *Miscellanies* deal with this happy prospect perhaps as some subconscious anticipation of going where he too would behold the church from a more glorious vista. An argument he gives that the saints in heaven are acquainted with what is done on earth is that God so often cites the ''notice the heavens shall take of these particular wonders of God's mercy and faithfulness.''[107]

But, are the saints in heaven unable to see the sins of the saints on earth? Is love truly blind so that where love is perfected the ability to perceive evil is destroyed? Is this why the contemplation of earth does not disturb the tranquility of heaven? No, the perfected saints are not blind, but they see how even the failings of the church militant work ultimately for God's glory and the church's own good, and that fills them with joy.

Of course, if the saints in glory recognize the saints on earth it certainly follows that when they too come to heaven they will be recognized. What about Edwards and the saints at Northampton who rejected him as their pastor? Understandably the ''Farewell Sermon''[108] does not dilate on theological niceties about whether the saints will recognize one another in heaven. That is assumed from the beginning, as the sermon opens with a general description of the day of judgment with the whole world assembled, yet with certain groups, such as the pastor and his former people, having a very special consciousness of one another. Edwards stresses the importance of the issues, the perfection of the Judge, and the efficiency of his judgment. He implies but does not say that there will be a separation between pastor and people.

They that evil entreat Christ's faithful ministers, especially in that wherein they are faithful, shall be severely punished; Matt. x. 14, 15. ''And whosoever shall not receive you, nor hear your words, when ye depart out of that house or city, shake off the dust of your feet. Verily I say unto you, it shall be more tolerable for the sinners of Sodom and Gomorrah, in the day of judgment, than for that city.

---

106. M1061. Hickman, II, 638.
107. M1121. Hickman, II, 640.
108. Cf. note 27, above.

But, Edwards concludes the paragraph: "On the other hand, those ministers who are found to have been unfaithful, shall have a most terrible punishment. See Ezek. xxxiii. 6. Matt. xxiii. 1-33."[109] So he seems to be affirming recognition indeed but separation in matters such as caused the division in Northampton. There is no hint that people will at the day of judgment see things differently and be somehow forgivable. The die seems to have been cast. There is no doubt that Edwards considered his own position in the controversy sound and faithful. Our point here is that the church in heaven, being aware of such controversies, must have understood the rights and wrongs, realized that God was working all things together for good in this world for those who loved him and vindication in the world to come.

The final touch is that the church in heaven is more interested in the church on earth than the church on earth is interested in the church on earth!

> The saints in heaven will be under advantages to see much more of it than the saints on earth and to be every way more directly fully and perfectly acquainted with all that appertains to it and that manifests the glory of it, the glory of God's wisdom and other perfections in it, the blessed fruit and end of it in the eternal glory and blessedness of the subjects of the work of God's at that day, will be daily in their view, in those that come out of dying bodies to heaven. And the church in heaven will be much more concerned in it, than one part of the church on earth shall be in the prosperity of another.[110]

Heaven Beholding Hell

". . . no occasion of grief to 'em but rejoicing."

"All things are yours" wrote Paul to the Corinthian saints (I Cor. 3:21). In Edwards's thought "all things" included hell.[111]

---

109. Hickman, I, ccxlv.
110. M1061.
111. Rev. 18:20, "When the saints in glory shall see the wrath of God executed on ungodly men, it will be no occasion of grief to 'em but of rejoicing" (p. 5), March 1733. Hickman, II, 210f., "the substance of two posthumous discourses (sic) dated March 1733."

Hell, like a gladiatorial combat, was made for the spectators not the participants. The sufferers were useful only in their suffering.[112] All blessing from this curse came to God and the godly. Since God cannot be made happier, being ever and infinitely blessed, hell was made, not for him but for heaven. Indeed, Edwards virtually reasons that heaven would not be heaven without hell. It is an argument for the fact of hell that heaven is blessed by it.

> I am convinced that hell torments will be eternal from [one great] good the wisdom of God proposes by them, which is by the sight of them to exalt the happiness, the love, and joyful thanksgivings of the angels and men that are saved, which it tends exceedingly to do. I am ready to think that those beholding the sight of the great miseries of those of their species that are damned will double the ardour of their love and the fulness of the joy of the elect angels and men.[113]

The rejoicing of the righteous over the suffering of the sinful is not sinful itself, because "the damned suffering divine vengeance will be no occasion of joy to the saints merely as tis others' misery or because that tis pleasant to them to behold others' misery merely for its own sake"[114] but as it revealed the justice and majesty of God. Still, there will be no pity because the glory of God will in their esteem be "of greater consequence than the welfare of thousands and millions of souls."[115]

This act of divine wrath exhibits the dreadful majesty, authority, justice, and holiness of God and thereby excites exquisite love in the saints. Since the happiness of the saints is to be double, the suffering of sinners must be eternal![116] "The misery of the damned in hell is one of those great things that the saints in their blessed and joyful state in heaven shall behold and take great notice of throughout eternity."[117]

"When the saints in glory shall see the wrath of God executed

---

112. Ezek. 15:2-4, "Mankind, if they bring forth no fruit to God are wholly useless unless it be in their destruction" (p. 3), July 1734. Cf. Prov. 19:4.

113. M279.

114. Rev. 18:20, pp. 10, 11.

115. *Ibid.*, p. 12.

116. Cf. M866, M491, and Rom. 9:22 (2), "God has no other use to put finally impenitent sinners to but only to suffer his wrath" (p. 3), Nov. 1741.

117. Isa. 66:23, June 1742, p. 1.

on ungodly men, it will be no occasion of grief to 'em, but of rejoicing."[118] Since this sermon is definitive and has been published we will follow its outline of our mind-boggling subject. Edwards sees this text (Rev. 18:20) as an account of the fall of Babylon, the antichristian, papal church. It has reference partly to the overthrow in this world and in the next. "But we are not to understand those plagues here mentioned as exclusive of the future vengeance that God will execute upon the wicked upholders and promoters of antichristianism and the cruel antichristian persecutors in another world."[119] The next chapter of Revelation, in fact, refers to the smoke rising "forever and ever." Of course, individual antichristians go to hell at death, but the text refers to a visible demonstration in this world and the world to come. At that time Antichrist is restricted to hell and has no more place on earth (cf. Rev. 20:1f.).[120] On this occasion, in our text, the apostles and prophets and the rest of the church triumphant are summoned to see God take vengeance on their enemies and oppressors.

All the enemies of the church through all the ages will be gathered and condemned together as directly or indirectly of the same company, "Satan's army."[121] The saints will rejoice because God is vindicating them. "Rejoice, for God hath avenged you on her." The Scriptures "plainly teach" that heaven will behold hell as Lazarus and Abraham saw Dives in his misery.[122] Isaiah 66:24, "And they shall go forth and look on the carcasses of the men that have transgressed against me: for their worm shall not die, neither shall their fire be quenched." Christ had taught that the sheep on his right hand at the judgment would see the wicked on his left hand and hear Christ say: "Depart, ye cursed, into everlasting fire, prepared for the devil and his angels." So the saints in heaven and sinners in hell shall some way or other have a direct and immediate apprehension of each other's state.[123]

This will be a terrible sight because God's wrath is meant to "make his power known." Better than now the saints will see

---

118. Rev. 18:20, March 1733.
119. *Ibid.*, p. 2.
120. *Ibid.*, p. 3.
121. *Ibid.*, p. 5.
122. *Ibid.*, p. 6.
123. *Ibid.*, p. 7.

and understand the divine anger poured out on the wicked, but it will cause no "uneasiness or unpleasantness to them."[124] Rather, "it will excite to joyful praises."[125]

Will this dreadful sight not cause grief in the sensitive righteous?[126] No, but their rejoicing is not from any "ill disposition"[127] in them. They are not called to "rejoice in having their revenge glutted but rejoice in seeing God's justice exercised."[128] Heaven will have no pity for hell, not because the saints are unloving, but because they are perfectly loving. They love as God loves and whom God loves, being now in perfect conformity with his love. "The glory of God" as we have seen, "in their esteem will be of greater consequence, than the welfare of thousands and millions of souls." They will therefore rejoice in the glory and power of God manifested in this holy and just manner.

The objection arises. If saints are to grieve now when men go to hell, why should they rejoice then?[129] Edwards gives five answers. First, it is the Christian's duty now to love even the wicked, not knowing but that they may be loved of God. In hell they are seen to be hated of God and so are hated by the saints.[130] Second, all men are now capable of salvation through the efforts of men but in hell salvation is past forever.[131] Third, rejoicing at calamities may now be because of envy and other evil dispositions, but in heaven saints rejoice only in the glory of God.[132] Fourth, natural affection "is no virtue in the saints in glory. Their virtue will exercise itself in a higher manner."[133] Fifth, when God takes vengeance on oppressors it is always because of his love to his saints; so in hell this infinite love for his own will be eternally visible in the punishment of their wicked enemies whom they love in this world.[134]

The sermon closes with a poignant and solemn warning to the

---

124. *Ibid.*, p. 8.
125. *Ibid.*
126. *Ibid.*, pp. 10f.
127. *Ibid.*, p. 10.
128. *Ibid.*, p. 11.
129. *Ibid.*, pp. 17f.
130. *Ibid.*, pp. 18, 19.
131. *Ibid.*, pp. 19, 20.
132. *Ibid.*, p. 20.
133. *Ibid.*
134. *Ibid.*, p. 21.

ungodly in Northampton.[135] References to parents delighting in the eternal torments of their own incorrigible children are moving. The congregation must have felt this paragraph especially:

> Consider ye that have long lived under Mr. Stoddard's ministry and are yet in a natural condition, how dreadful it will be to you to see him that was so tenderly concerned for the good of your souls while here and so earnestly sought your salvation, to see him rising up in judgment against you, declaring your inexcusableness, declaring how often he warned you. How will you feel, when you shall see him approving the sentence of condemnation that the Judge shall pronounce against you.... And when you shall see him rejoicing in the execution of justice upon you for all your unprofitableness under his ministry![136]

Some today imagine that the loving character of God and saints would seem to rule hell out. Hell would seem to make them miserable—make heaven into hell. We see, however, that so far from making holy beings miserable, hell actually makes them happy. It is obvious that this would have to be so because the ever-blessed God eternally knows perfectly of the hell which he himself ordains. Saints, even in this world, are informed of the present existence of hell. Edwards is only articulating in his characteristically thorough manner, what the Bible plainly teaches, and all Bible believers must necessarily accept. "This is life eternal" says Jesus Christ, "that they know thee the only true God . . ." (John 17:3). The only true God, according to Jonathan Edwards, sends sinners to, and torments them in, hell. Eternal life depends on knowing, accepting, trusting in, the God who does this.

It is a great hurdle for many even to accept, much less find pleasure in, this doctrine. But here in Revelation 18:20 Edwards is showing that far more than that is characteristic of a saint. The torments of the damned "will be no occasion of grief to 'em, but of rejoicing." Christians, imperfectly now and perfectly hereafter, will be made happy by the sight of *justified* misery.

If the temptation arises to feign pleasure, no student of Edwards would succumb. He would know that feigning is futile in

---

135. *Ibid.*, pp. 21-34.
136. *Ibid.*, pp. 28, 29.

the presence of the Searcher of Hearts. That would make the feigner twofold more the child of hell than open rebellion would. The bottom line is not that a good person must constrainedly acquiesce and rejoice in the contemplation of hell but that he will do so spontaneously and naturally. There is no sadism here because the torment is deserved. Not a cruel man but a good man rejoices in just punishment. It is sadism *not* to rejoice in just misery. Why? Sadism is pleasure in suffering for suffering's sake. The person either rejoices in just suffering or he does not. That is, he either rejoices in hell or does not. If he does not rejoice in hell he rejoices in no-hell. The no-hell in which we now live has much unjust suffering. That person, therefore, who does not rejoice in hell prefers the world that now is to hell (because hell is God's only cure for incorrigible wickedness). He acquiesces in and enjoys unjust suffering, and that is sadism. The seeming ''sentimentalist'' is therefore the true sadist, and the rejoicer in just punishment is the true lover of the souls of men. Edwards's sermon concludes with a sustained and passionate appeal to repent and be saved from hell and to God.

The Eternality of Heaven

''The heavenly inhabitants . . . remain in eternal youth.''

One of Edwards's very earliest sermons was a strong apologetic for immortality. ''All men must certainly die and after death their everlasting state will be determined.''[137] This is proven not only by revelation but by natural reason and conscience as well. The wicked do prosper and the righteous do suffer in this world, necessitating a future judgment. Edwards said that all nations agree, including the ''barbarously ignorant indians here in America,''[138] that the ''soul will endure forever.'' In this sermon young Edwards is arguing in the classic fashion that though reason convinces, the Bible ''puts it past doubt.'' What puts the Bible

137. Heb. 9:27 (1), p. 2, between 1721 and 1722.
138. *Ibid.*, p. 10.

past doubt is miracle because "one true miracle is a demonstration of the truth for which it is wrought."[139]

The truth of an immortality of rewards and punishment is absolutely fundamental. If there are no everlasting states "then the whole of religion is immediately thrown up and destroyed."[140] The case is demonstrative, and unbelievers will be "enveloped in hell's flames."[141] And they have "danger of dropping into the bottomless pit every moment."[142] Thus, early in his ministry, Edwards is already complaining that people are insensitive to hell, unafraid though they are going there. They allow all warning to bounce off "as a ball from a marble wall."[143]

That the eternity of the future state of happiness and misery spoken of in Scripture is a proper eternity, "absolutely excluding any end, is most clearly manifest by Luke 20:36—neither can they die anymore—and other places. Rev. 21.4...."[144] Many more texts are cited to prove the same point with the main emphasis on the eternality of heaven as the "last enemy," death, is conquered. "The heavenly inhabitants do as it were remain in eternal youth."[145]

The rather abstruse concept of eternity is carefully probed by Edwards even in his sermons, probably because, however recondite the subject, it is of immediate interest and concern for sinner and saint alike, the one hoping immortality is not a fact and the other rejoicing that it is.

While the sermon on II Corinthians 4:18 asserts that "there is such a thing as eternity,"[146] that on Romans 6:23 asks what eternity is[147] and then proceeds to show that there is such a thing as eternity awaiting every man. First, nature shows that there must be immortal existence following the inevitable judgment of rewards and punishments for deeds done in this world. But leaving deism far behind, Edwards's second point is that special

---

139. *Ibid.*, p. 13.
140. *Ibid.*, p. 14.
141. *Ibid.*, p. 18.
142. Sermon (2), p. 11.
143. *Ibid.*, p. 12.
144. M1004.
145. Mark 16:5. Quarterly Lecture, Nov. 1747, p. 2.
146. Sermon (2), p. 1. April 1742.
147. "1. What is eternal life. 2. How eternal life is the gift of God. 3. How it is God's gift through Jesus Christ" (p. 1), Nov. 1746, March 1754.

revelation is necessary to show clearly what immortality is and what will bring a blessed immortality. And this is precisely what the gospel of Jesus Christ has brought to light.

Showing that there is such a thing as eternity, Edwards begins the II Corinthians 4:18 sermon by attempting a definition. The word is sometimes used as that without beginning, sometimes of that without end. "God is possessed of the whole at once."[148] It is essentially "incomprehensible" and we can only try to imagine it.[149] So, what then is meant by the word? "That there is an eternal state. . . ."[150] However difficult to define, Edwards finds it relatively easy to prove. For one thing, the "light of nature teaches the immortality of the soul"[151] and also teaches that revelation is necessary to show how to "escape misery" and "obtain happiness."[152] This was "brought to light" by Christ, who "confirmed his word by many miracles."[153]

On the basis of revelation, Edwards shows what eternity will be. In sum, "God will be the hell of one and the heaven of the other."[154] In eternity all things will be brought to their term and fixed. In that world no mixture of good and evil will be found.[155] Then follows an unusual application in which he points out the comforts in the eternity of the one and the misery for the other.[156] "Improve the time to make sure [of heaven]."[157]

It is to be noted that Edwards's immortality implies a conferred immutability. Only God is, *per se,* immutable. Because he is so, he can and does preserve rational creatures in the state they are at death, to the perfect degree. For the saints this means eternal heaven.

It is interesting that while the deists loosened their grip on eternity, Edwards strengthened his. It was no mystery why the "immortal deists" gave way to the "mortal deists" as Edwards's grip on eternity tightened. The deists were understanding more

---

148. II Cor. 4:18 (2), p. 2.
149. *Ibid.,* pp. 2, 3.
150. *Ibid.,* p. 4.
151. *Ibid.*
152. *Ibid.*
153. *Ibid.*
154. *Ibid.,* p. 5.
155. *Ibid.,* pp. 5, 6.
156. *Ibid.,* pp. 7–20.
157. *Ibid.,* p. 20.

and more why Hume had said that the arguments they used to destroy supernatural revelation were fatal to natural revelation. With the rejection of the God of special revelation went, as a matter of historical, if not logical, fact, the immortality of natural revelation. The deists unwittingly proved Edwards's point in M1340: "reason no substitute for revelation."[158] "To him that hath (special revelation) it shall be given (the confirmation of natural revelation) and to him that hath not (special revelation) shall be taken that which he thinks he hath (natural revelation)."

╱The Rationale of Heaven

"Then God will fully have glorified himself. . . ."

In a sense, *The Dissertation on the Last End of God in the Creation of the World* is the rationale for heaven. If God's chief end is his manifestative glory, as the treatise maintains,[159] where is that fully realized so well as in heaven? We will see that God's glory is realized also in hell but more indirectly and as a "strange" rather than natural work. Hell is used by the saints in heaven as an occasion for the glorification of God, to be sure. But, it is heaven where God's true glory is realized in and by its inhabitants. If this is so, then, for Edwards, the purpose or rationale of heaven is precisely that there can be no higher end.

In M371,[160] where Edwards recapitulates what happens in heaven at the resurrection, he is, in a sense, giving the rationale for heaven. First, "the saints will be in their natural state of union with bodies, glorious bodies, bodies perfectly fitted for the uses of a holy glorified soul."[161] This is man's natural state that has been temporarily interrupted in the intermediate or "separate state." Man was created body and soul and is destined to be such forever. So at the resurrection he reaches his natural state in a glorified condition, body and soul together. This is the ultimate destiny of the elect fully realized only in heaven.

---

158. Hickman, I, 94ff.
159. *Ibid.*
160. Hickman, II, 620; M371.
161. *Ibid.*

Second,

> then the body of Christ will be perfect; the church will be complete; all the parts of it in being; no parts of it under sin or affliction; all the parts of it in a perfect [state]; all the parts of it together no longer mixed with ungodly men; then the church will be as a bride adorned for her husband, therefore the church will exceedingly rejoice.[162]

Thus, not only the perfect state of the individual is realized but the perfect state of the entire body of Christ.

The communion of the saints in the fulness of its ideal is now in heaven a reality. The church in this world possesses this communion in principle but most imperfectly. In the intermediate state the souls of just men are made perfect but they are still disembodied and to that degree imperfect or, at least, unnatural. Only in heaven does the striving of the ages and the longing of all the saints come to its ultimate fruition. Not only are the spots and wrinkles of the bride of Christ herself removed, but the disfiguring presence of these who do not truly belong to her company is removed. Only the bride in all her loveliness is present for the wedding ceremony, which can take place only when she has been made fit for her divine husband. This is manifestly the supreme goal of the church; her very raison d'être.

Third,

> then the Mediator will have fully accomplished his work; will have destroyed, and will triumph over all his enemies. Then Christ will fully have obtained his reward. Then shall be perfected the full design that was upon his heart from all eternity, and then Jesus Christ will rejoice, and his members must needs rejoice with him.[163]

So the rationale of heaven is the fruition of the destiny not only of the redeemed but of the Redeemer himself as well. Only in heaven is the full triumph of Christ achieved. This is the grand climax of all his work and the purpose for it all. Were it not for heaven, the goal of redemption would not have been obtained and

---

162. *Ibid.*
163. *Ibid.*

failing that all would have been in vain. That alone would be sufficient reason to establish heaven securely forever. Fourth,

> then God will have obtained the end of all his great works that he had been doing from the beginning; then all the deep designs of God will be unfolded in their events; then the wisdom of his marvellous contrivances in his hidden, intricate, and inexplicable works will appear, the ends being obtained; then God's glory will more abundantly appear in his works, his works being perfect. This will cause a great accession of happiness to the saints who behold it; then God will fully have glorified himself, and glorified his Son, and his elect; then he will see that all is very good, and will rejoice in his own works, which will be the joy of all heaven. God will rest and be refreshed; and thenceforward will the inhabitants keep an eternal sabbath, such an one as all foregoing sabbaths were but shadows of.[164]

Here is where Edwards himself virtually attributes to heaven the role of being the end for which God created the world. All his contrivances and wisdom are seen here in their outworking. The items which have preceded and the ones that follow are but steps in that direction. Heaven is the name of the game. All of God's roads lead to heaven. That is what Aristotle would have called God's final cause. All material, efficient, and instrumental causes were subordinate to this final cause. Heaven, in a sense, is the end not only of all man's striving but of all God's "striving." Finally,

> then God will make more abundant manifestations of his glory, and of the glory of his Son, and will pour forth more plentifully of his Spirit, and will make answerable additions to the glory of the saints, as will be becoming the commencement of the ultimate and most perfect state of things, and as will become such a joyful occasion as the finishing of all things and the marriage of the Lamb. Then also the glory of the angels will receive proportional additions; for as the evil angels are then to have the consummation of their reward, so then the good angels will have the consummation of their reward. This will be the day of Christ's triumph, and the day will last forever. This will be the wedding-day between Christ and the church, and this wedding-day will never end. The

---

164. *Ibid.*

feast, and pomp, and entertainments, and holy mirth, and joys of the wedding will be continued to all eternity.[165]

One wondered how even Edwards could excel this fourth point. But anything less than an everlasting celebration would have been an eternal let-down. Union with Christ simply could not be perfect if the saints ever had to contemplate its end. They would dread every passing day with Jesus knowing that it brought them ever closer to eternal separation. The love of the saints could not let Christ go, but, even if it could, this fifth point reminds the church that his love will never let her go.

The Objections to Heaven

". . . here providence will not suffer any great degree of happiness."

One would suppose that there would be no objections to heaven. But Edwards makes his own objection. He gives an argument that he has produced out of sheer reflection, looking, as it were, in the corners of his mind for anything hiding there. In M585 he says:

It has sometimes looked strange to me, that men should be ever brought to such exceeding happiness as that of heaven seems to be, because we find that here providence won't suffer any great degree of happiness. When men have something in which they hope to find very great joy, there will be something to spoil it. Providence seems watchfully to take care that [men] should have no exceeding joy and satisfaction here in this world. But indeed this, instead of being an argument against the greatness of heaven's happiness, seems to argue for it; for we can't suppose that the reason why providence won't suffer men to enjoy great happiness here is, that he is averse to the creature's happiness, but because this is not a time for it. To every thing there is an appointed season and time. And 'tis agreeable to God's method of dispensation that a thing should be sought in vain out of its appointed time. God reserves happiness to be bestowed hereafter;

---

165. *Ibid.*

that is the appointed time for it, and that is the reason he don't give it now. No man, let him be never so strong or wise, shall alter this divine establishment, by anticipating happiness before his appointed time. 'Tis so in all things: sometimes there is an appointed time for a man's prosperity upon earth, and then nothing can hinder their prosperity; and then when that time is past, then comes an appointed time for his adversity, and then all things conspire for his ruin, and all his strength and skill shall not help him. . . .

In other words, Edwards's view of divine theodicy is that the very frustrations of this life, so far from arguing frustrations as the perpetual lot of man, intimate that there must be a place called heaven where things are different. Man's heart is restless until it finds its rest in thee, said Augustine. Man's heart is restless, therefore it must find its rest in thee, said Edwards. Although he does not mention it in this *Miscellany* Edwards was no doubt thinking that this is a fallen world in which sorrow and death are as natural as their absence would be in a world of virtue and light. So, that which first appears as an objection to, is a major argument for, heaven. As a matter of fact, at one point Edwards seems to think that the injustice of this world, with its need for correction in another world, is the only valid argument for immortality.[166] That would mean that the very hellishness of this world is an argument for heaven in the armory of natural theology.

The Beatific Vision

"The saints in heaven shall see God."[167]

The ultimate glory is not in seeing friends in heaven, not even in seeing the glorified Son of Man, the very light of heaven. The ultimate glory is the view of God himself; the beatific vision; the

---

166. Hickman, II, 477.
167. M1134. The sermon on Isa. 33:17, June 1736, has this theme: "They that are the true subjects and sincere and faithful servants of Jesus Christ shall be admitted to see their King in his beauty," p. 5.

amor intellectualis Dei. Among all the ecstasies of glory none
was more important for Jonathan Edwards than the perfect
intellectual-spiritual vision of God.
Nevertheless, this is a very rare experience even in heaven.
Generally, the beatific vision is a view of the exalted and
glorified Christ. This, for example, is Edwards's way of describing it in M777:

> ... that *beatifical vision* that the saints have of God in heaven is in
> beholding the manifestations that he makes of himself in the work
> of redemption. For that arguing of the being and perfections of
> God that may be *a priori* don't seem to be called seeing God in
> Scripture, but only that which is by manifestations God makes of
> himself in his Son. All other ways of knowing God are by seeing
> him in Christ the Redeemer, the image of the invisible God, and
> in his works; or, the effects of his perfections in his redemption
> and the fruits of it (which effects are the principal manifestation or
> shining forth of his perfections). And in conversing with them by
> Christ which conversation is chiefly about those things done and
> manifested in this work, if we may judge by the subject of God's
> conversation with his church by his word in this world. And so we
> may infer that business and employment of the saints so far as it
> consists in contemplation, praise & conversation is mainly in
> contemplating the wonders of this work, in praising God for the
> displays of his glory and love therein, and in conversing about
> things appertaining to it.

Perhaps Edwards's most explicit and fuller definition of the
beatific vision occurs in the sermon on Romans 2:10. "Glory,
honor, and peace is the portion that God has given to all the
godly." In the concluding part of this sermon he describes the
nature and degree of the consummate and eternal glory and blessedness of the saints. He begins "with the lowest part of it, viz.
the glory of the place."[168] Item by item he pursues his celestial
theme telling of the glory of the bodies of the saints and of their
fellowship with one another. Only finally does he arrive, in this
path of ecstasy, to the supreme glory of heaven, the beatific
vision itself. Let us listen to his homiletic rhapsody:

> The saints in heaven shall see God. ... This is that which is called
> by divines "the beatific vision," because this is that which the

168. P. 60.

blessedness of the saints in glory does chiefly consist in. This is
the highest part of their blessedness. Now we are come to the
fountain, the infinite fountain of blessedness. The sight of Christ
which has already been spoken of is not here to be excluded
because he is a divine person. The sight of him in his divine nature
therefore belongs to the beatifical vision. The vision of God is the
heaven of heaven. And therefore I would speak to it a little particularly.

I would consider the faculty that is the immediate subject of this
vision. It is no sight of any thing with the bodily eyes but it is an
intellectual view. The beatifical vision of God is not a sight with
the eyes of the body, but with the eye of the soul. There is no such
thing as seeing God properly with the bodily [eyes] because he is a
spirit; one of his attributes is, that he is invisible. . . . This highest
blessedness of the soul does not enter in at the door of the bodily
senses: this would be to make the blessedness of the soul dependent on the body, or the happiness of man's superior part to be
dependent on the inferior. The beatifical vision of God is not any
sight with the bodily eyes, because the separate souls of the saints,
and the angels which are mere spirits, and never were united to
body, have this vision. . . . 'Tis not in beholding any form of
visible representation, or shape, or colour, or shining light, that
the highest happiness of the soul consists in; but 'tis in seeing God,
who is a spirit, spiritually, with the eyes of the soul.

We have no reason to think that there is any such thing as God's
manifesting himself by any outward glorious appearance, that is,
the symbol of his presence in heaven, any otherwise than by the
glorified body of Christ. God was wont, under the Old Testament,
oftentimes to manifest himself by an outward glory, and sometimes in an outward shape, or the form of a man. But when God
manifested himself thus, it was by Christ; it was the second person
of the Trinity only that was wont thus to appear to men in an
outward glory and human shape. . . . But since Christ has actually
assumed a human body there is no need of his assuming any aerial
form or shape any more. He is now become visible to the bodily
eyes in a more perfect manner by his having a real body.

The saints that shall see Christ in heaven in his glorified body,
do much more properly see Christ than if they only saw an assumed shape, or some outward glorious appearance, as the symbol of his presence; for now, that which they see is not only a
glorious appearance by which Christ is represented but the real
Christ; 'tis his own body. The seeing God in the glorified body of
Christ is the most perfect way of seeing God with the bodily eyes
that can be; for in seeing a real body that one of the persons of the
Trinity has assumed to be his body, and that he dwells in for ever
as his own in which the divine majesty and excellency appears as

much as 'tis possible for it to appear in outward form or shape. The saints do actually see a divine person with bodily eyes, and in the same manner as we see one another. But when God showed himself under outward appearances and symbols of his presence only, that was not so proper a sight of a divine person. It was a more imperfect way of God's manifesting himself suitable to the more imperfect state of the church under the Old Testament. But now Christ does really subsist in a glorified body; those outward symbols and appearances are done away as being needless and imperfect. . . . [169]

Edwards continues with further details and reaches his climax with these words: "They shall see everything in God that tends to excite and inflame love, i.e., every thing that is lovely, every thing that tends to exalt their esteem and admiration, to warm and endear the heart. . . . They shall see every thing in God that gratifies love. . . . " The effect of this vision is "that the soul hereby shall be inflamed with love and satisfied with pleasure . . . " [170]

---

169. Rom. 2:10, pp. 81–84. (We have deleted the many biblical quotations on which the statements are based.)
170. *Ibid.*, pp. 85–90.

2
Hell

"This doctrine is indeed awful and dreadful yet tis of God."

In 1962 Clarence H. Faust wrote: "It is true that Edwards was much more than a sensational preacher of hell-fire sermons, but no fully rounded picture of the man can disregard this aspect of his work."[1] It is evident that the present revival of interest in the "puritan sage" has not denied this aspect of Edwards but neither Faust nor the contemporary concern has done justice to Edwards's emphasis on this theme.

Our age will not stand as much of hell as his own, and even it complained. Edwards wore himself out as he had said that Stoddard had done before him. In a 1747 sermon he laments:

> And indeed when I went about preparing this discourse it was with considerable discouragement. I thought it was now some time since I had offered any discourse of this nature. But so many had been offered with so little apparent effect that I thought with myself I know not what to say further.
>
> But however because I must warn you from God whether you will hear or whether you will forbear I have warned you again. It has now been told once more, whether you will yield to the power of God's Word, to the force of the awful warnings and threatenings which the Word of God sets before you [or not]. If you will not hear now you may possibly solemnly lay these things to heart when you come to die. And if you continue in your stupidity to the last, being given up of God to a dreadful degree of hardness that is beyond the alarm of approaching death, which is the case with some, yet as soon as ever you are dead you will be fully sensible of all.[2]

---

1. Faust and Thomas H. Johnson, *Jonathan Edwards: Representative Selections . . .* , rev. ed. (New York: Hill and Wang, 1962), p. xxiii.
2. Exod. 9:12-16, July 1747, pp. 42, 43. Cf. also Isa. 33:14 (2), Dec. 1740, at Stockbridge and to Stockbridge Indians. Hickman, II, 201f.; Worcester, rev., IV, 488f. "The time will come when fearfulness will surprise the sinners in Zion because they will know that they are going to be cast into a devouring fire which they must suffer forever and ever, and which none can endure" (p. 45). Cf. Ezek. 22:14, "(1) Since God has undertaken to deal with impenitent sinners they shall neither shun the threatened misery nor deliver themselves out of it, nor can they bear it" (p. 3), April 1741 and May 1753, Mohawks. Hickman, II, 78f.; Worcester, rev., IV, 489f. Cf. also this lament from the 1730 sermon on Mark 9:44: Edwards says his people were "told from Sabbath to Sabbath of eternal misery" (p. 28). Still, they would not be stirred up or think about it. He continues:

It was this great ever-present danger that drove Edwards to warn his generation so often. "'Tis a dreadful thing but yet a common thing for persons to go to hell.'"[3] This will be among the laments of the damned.[4]

After the spiritual drought following the awakening of 1734–35, God was pleased to pour out his Spirit again in 1740,[5] when Edwards observed: "If it should always have continued as it has been for five or six years past almost all of you would surely have gone to hell. . . ."[6] Still, not everyone was being converted. "It is an awful thing to think of that there are now some persons in this very congregation, here and there, in one seat and another that will be the subjects of that very misery that we have now heard of as dreadful as it is though it be so intolerable and though it be eternal.'"[7] The closing dirge: "tell 'em of hell as often as you will and set it out in as lively colours as you will, they will be slack and slothful.'"[8]

Yet, we know that not all who heard Edwards were unconvinced.[9] Some were even converted. There were still others who were neither despisers nor converts. Of them, he says that "they were neither awakened, nor at ease.'"[10]

Overall, Edwards's distribution of sermons, which it is virtually impossible to classify precisely, may not run three to one in favor of minatory to comforting themes (as the Bible itself seems to do), but it certainly favors such an emphasis. As a rough sample check we found among the 140 sermons on Matthew 13 devoted explicitly to heaven, 23 to hell. Of the 43 Mark sermons there were 7 on heaven and 4 on hell. Luke's 111 had 10 on heaven and 13 on hell.

"You'll see it amongst many middle-aged persons and so it is still with many when advanced in years and they certainly draw near to the grave." "And yet those same persons will seem to acknowledge that the greater part of men go to hell and suffer eternal misery and that through their carelessness about it, but yet they'll do the same" (pp. 28, 29).

3. I Cor. 11:32, Aug. 1741, p. 2.

4. Prov. 5:11, "Subject, the mourning of sinners in another world," at Sargt. Allyns, March 31, 1751, and 1751 St. Ind. (Andover Collection).

5. Isa. 33:14 (2), p. 39, "God is pleased again to be pouring out his spirit upon us and he is doing great things amongst [us]."

6. *Ibid.*, p. 40.

7. *Ibid.*, p. 42.

8. *Ibid.*, p. 44.

9. *Ibid.*, p. 12.

10. This sentiment was expressed frequently in Edwards's preaching.

It is to be remembered furthermore that Edwards does not use texts as pretexts or even as mere points of departure for a topical development. He almost always begins with a contextual introduction and then proceeds to expound the meaning of his text, which he then states in the form of a "doctrine." So when Edwards devotes these sermons to hell, he believes that the texts deal with that subject and that it is incumbent on him as a steward of the mysteries of God to do the same. However many *Miscellanies* deal directly or indirectly with this subject, Edwards, in his own table of contents, lists more than sixty.

The Nature of Hell

"Tis the infinite almighty God that shall become the fire of the furnace."

Hell is a spiritual and material furnace of fire where its victims are exquisitely tortured in their minds and in their bodies eternally, according to their various capacities, by God, the devils, and damned humans including themselves, in their memories and consciences as well as in their raging, unsatisfied lusts, from which place of death God's saving grace, mercy, and pity are gone forever, never for a moment to return. Edwards nowhere gives such a comprehensive definition, but this is the way we put his message together as his overall view of hell, to which he gave so much reflection in his study and in his pulpit. Perhaps it should be recalled here that God had, according to Edwards, ordained many humans and devils to this awful destiny in accord with their own moral choices, and that fact had been viewed by him originally as "horrid" doctrine, his conversion occurring only when he experienced the beauty of its truth.[11]

Commenting on Matthew 13:47-50 (1), "The wicked will hereafter be cast into a furnace of fire,"[12] Edwards notes that "furnace of fire" is a common and most apt biblical representa-

---

11. Faust and Johnson, *op. cit.*, pp. 57f. Cf. D. B. Shea, Jr., "The Art and Instruction of Jonathan Edwards's *Personal Narrative*" in S. Bercovich, ed., *The American Puritan Imagination* (London: Cambridge University Press, 1974), p. 165.

12. P. 1, June 1746.

tion of future punishment. Many times in this sermon and elsewhere he uses this metaphor. In the Romans 2:8, 9[13] message he referred to the "deluge of fire," preaching that when the day of judgment comes, the wicked shall rise to the resurrection of damnation.[14] "It will be a dreadful sight to them when they come to their bodies again, those bodies which were formerly approved by them as the organs and instruments of sin and wickedness . . . and they shall very unwillingly enter into them."[15] Indeed, these bodies will be "loathsome and hideous."[16] In this condition "they shall have nothing to do to spend away their eternity but to conflict with these torments."[17]

In the Ezekiel 22:14 (2) sermon Edwards speaks again of the great furnace of fire.[18] Using the "rhetoric of sensation" even more explicitly, he depicts the furnace as heated "by degrees" and describes the humans being eternally destroyed after the simile of the spider in the flame. In addition to the furnace metaphor Edwards frequently uses the expressions "lake of fire,"[19] "conflagration,"[20] "burnt in hell."[21]

Is this furnace spiritual or material? It is both. In the same sermon which notes that "furnace of fire" is the most common biblical symbol,[22] Edwards addresses the question whether the furnace is metaphorical or material. It may be understood either literally or figuratively, he reasons. Figuratively speaking, the wrath of God is a consuming fire. Dives in torment spiritually, even before the resurrection of his body, was described as in fire, begging to have Lazarus wet his tongue to relieve the pain. The metaphor points to the all-over prevalence of the anguish and its

---

13. "Indignation, wrath, and misery and anguish of soul is the portion that God has allotted to wicked men" (p. 4), Nov. 1735. Hickman, II, 878f.; Dwight, VIII, 195f.

14. *Ibid.*, p. 31.

15. *Ibid.*, p. 32.

16. *Ibid.*, p. 33.

17. *Ibid.*, p. 41.

18. "When God comes to punish wicked men for their sins their heart cannot endure it" (p. 1), St. Ind., May 1753, Moh.

19. M275.

20. *Ibid.*

21. Rom. 3:19, p. 241. Cf. note 196 below.

22. Rev. 21:8 (1)–(3), "I would show how or in what is represented to us by the wicked's hereafter being cast into a lake of fire and brimstone. 2. How it is said that they shall have their part in it. 3. Why this is called the second death. 4. And lastly, I would warn all from thence to take heed. . . ." (p. 3). Jan. 1744–45.

intolerable severity. Divine wrath will be far more terrible than its symbol.

But the symbol is also "very probably" literal. Actually the furnace is figurative so far as the soul is concerned, literal as it pertains to the body. There is nothing impossible about its being literal, and Christ's words in Matthew 10:28 require it. After all, it takes real fire to burn the heavens and earth in the great conflagration, which is hell. Therefore that it will be literal fire is evident.[23] It will be more obviously literal after the day of judgment.[24] The bodies of the wicked will be cast into a "lake of liquid fire."[25] This doctrine is clear from reason as well as Scripture and from the traditions of the heathen. Commenting on the brazen images heated to white heat, in which ancient Israelites sometimes "passed" their children to the heathen god, Molech, Edwards surmises that these images were probably "not unlike" hell.[26] "'Tis probable that this earth after the conflagration shall be the place of the damned . . . many thousand times hotter than ordinary fire."[27] "The Scripture is plain that that great fire will be that in which the wicked will suffer to all eternity."[28] Later, Edwards calls the world after the conflagration a "universal wreck."[29] It will be the wicked's "fixed abode."[30]

Edwards finds much support for "literal" hell-fire. Comparing the suffering of hell to the agony of Christ in the Garden of Gethsemane (which caused him to sweat great drops of blood), Edwards justifies the torments of the damned being "literally as great as they are represented by fire and brimstone. . . ."[31] The sermon on Matthew 10:28 goes most particularly into the question of physical and spiritual torture in hell. "The bodies of wicked men as well as their souls will be punished forever in hell."[32]

In a careful analysis, Edwards observes that pain is only in the

---

23. *Ibid.*, p. 9.
24. *Ibid.*
25. *Ibid.*
26. Matt. 5:22, pp. 3f.
27. M275.
28. Rev. 21:8 (1)–(3), p. 14.
29. Hickman, II, 883.
30. Cf. section below entitled "The Locality of Hell."
31. M280.
32. Before 1733.

soul.[33] What is meant by "bodily pain" is that which is conveyed by the organs of the body.[34] Spiritual pain refers to that which comes directly from the soul's reflections.[35] It is fit that man should suffer in body and soul because he was created such and sinned in both.[36] In hell man is deprived of all pleasure derived through the sense; in fact, he is tormented through each sense (hearing, seeing, feeling).[37] Still the torments of the soul will be greater. The devils suffer only in soul, but, even so, more than men. The application of this sermon exhorts the wicked to give up seeking pleasure. The clothing which you so much covet now will be a cloak of fire in hell hereafter. A very practical direction follows the lament ("you have been told hundreds of times what you must do"):[38] You must give yourself body and soul to Christ.

The reason the great furnace is material and spiritual and incomparably more than a furnace or a lake of fire or even a conflagration is that it is really God himself. What are all these representations when we consider that "'tis the infinite almighty God himself that shall become the fire [of] the furnace exerting his infinite perfections that way."[39] "The appearance of the presence of an angry God in them and everywhere round about them, can be represented by nothing better than by their being in the midst of an exceedingly hot and furious fire. . . . " All this will be aggravated by the remembrance that God once loved them so as to give his Son to invite them to the happiness of his love.[40] The "spiritual" fire consists largely in this sense of "their being perfectly hated of God."[41] God feels this antagonism while the

---

33. *Ibid.,* p. 5.
34. *Ibid.,* pp. 6f.
35. *Ibid.,* p. 6.
36. *Ibid.,* pp. 8f.
37. *Ibid.,* pp. 14f. "The body will be full of torment as full as it can hold, and every part of it shall be full of torment. They shall be in extreme pain, every joint of 'em, every nerve shall be full of inexpressible torment. They shall be tormented even to their fingers' ends. The whole body shall be full of the wrath of God. Their hearts and their bowels and their heads, their eyes and their tongues, their hands and their feet will be filled with the fierceness of God's wrath. This is taught us in many Scriptures. . . . " (p. 15).
38. *Ibid.,* p. 24.
39. Job 41:9, 10, "We may in some measure judge how much more terrible the fierceness of God's wrath is than that of creatures by the difference there is between him and them" (p. 1), Jan. 1742–43, p. 11.
40. M232.
41. M592.

impenitent are in this world, but the stupidity[42] which desensitizes them here is removed hereafter. "In hell is inflicted the fierceness of the wrath of a being that is almighty" is the theme of the Revelation 19:15 sermon.[43] How they are hated and loathed by God![44] Even before you come under his wrath "it may be," preached Edwards, that "God has appointed you to the slaughter."[45]

The all-important feature of heaven and of hell is God himself. He is the one who makes heaven, heaven. He is the one who makes hell, hell. Indeed, according to Edwards, he is hell and he is heaven. Eternity for sinner and saint will be spent "in the immediate presence and sight of God...."[46] Preached Edwards: "God will be the hell of one and the heaven of the other."[47]

It is because God is the fire which burns in hell that words can never convey—much less exaggerate—the terrors of the damned. "Who can know the power of his anger?" asked the psalmist. Edwards took this to be a rhetorical question. "The law and the gospel both," he insisted, "agree that God intends an extraordinary manifestation of his terribleness."[48] If this be so, it was inevitable that Edwards would assuredly advise: "Let not the sinner imagine that these things are bugbears."[49] Future punishment is contrary neither to Scripture nor reason. In fact, it is most reasonable to suppose it.[50] He gives five arguments to prove that ministers have not "set it out beyond what it really is."[51] He then concludes confidently: "If I have set it [forth] too much then the Scripture has too which is blasphemous."[52]

It is interesting to hear the man whom all America and perhaps

---

42. Exod. 9:12-16, p. 43.

43. P. 4, April 1734. This sermon includes a three-point argument that God will never have pity on hell (pp. 12f.).

44. Luke 16:25 (1) and (2), "I. Wicked men in hell will remember how things were with them here in this world" (p. 3). "II. The wicked in hell will be sensible what a happy state the saints are in [in] heaven" (p. 2). Before 1733 and Sept. 1757. Cf. sermon on Heb. 12:29 (1), "God is a consuming fire" (p. 3), Aug. 1731-Dec. 1732. (2) "God himself is the fire that shall destroy and consume wicked men" (p. 1), May 1742.

45. Rom. 1:24, "God sometimes punishes sin by giving men up to sin," n.d., p. 11.

46. II Cor. 4:18 (2), "There is such a thing as eternity" (p. 1), April 1742, p. 5.

47. *Ibid.*

48. Job 41:9f., p. 15.

49. *Ibid.*

50. *Ibid.*

51. Rom. 2:8, 9, p. 50.

52. *Ibid.*, p. 56.

the world thinks so grossly overstated the anger of God against the sinners in his hand, confess: "After we have said our utmost and thought our utmost, all that we have said or thought is but a faint shadow of what really is."[53]

Although God is the misery of hell as he is the joy of heaven, the damned souls contribute to their own misery and not to one another's relief. They have no more friends in hell than they have in heaven. Instead of the damned being comforted in each other's company, it is probable that they will be as coals or brands in the fire that heat and burn one another. This is spelled out in the sermon on Matthew 13:30[54] in which Edwards says that so far from other wicked persons being a comfort, they will "greatly augment" each other's misery and torment as they detest, hate, and condemn one another. "They will perfectly and extremely hate one another."[55] If, as George Bernard Shaw and others have claimed, all the interesting people will be in hell, they will have no interest in one another except to torture. Even Lewis's *Great Divorce,* suggesting the loneliness of souls in hell, is understatement if, as Edwards represents it, they only add to the torment by their presence. In hell misery hates company.

The devils' thing is to inflict torture on the poor human sinners whom God hands over to them. One of the horrors Edwards drew for the congregations of *"Sinners in the Hands of an Angry God"* was that

> the devil stands ready to fall upon them and seize them as his own, at what moment God shall permit him. They belong to him; he has their souls in his possession, and under his dominion. . . . The devils watch them; they are ever by them . . . they stand waiting for them, like greedy hungry lions. . . . The old serpent is gaping for them; hell opens its mouth wide to receive them. . . .[56]

---

53. *Ibid.,* p. 53.
54. Matt. 13:30, May 1743. "Wicked men will have no comfort or relief by having company in hell but on the contrary they will greatly augment each other's misery and torment" (p. 1), May 1743, p. 6.
55. *Ibid.,* p. 3. This sermon also says that "they will be most ghastly and terrible sights one to another" (p. 3). "They will be strong to torment one another" (p. 5).
56. *Sinners in the Hands of an Angry God.* "A Sermon Preached at Enfield, July 8th, 1741. At a time of great Awakenings; and attended with remarkable Impressions on many of the Hearers. Boston, Printed: Edinburgh, Reprinted by T. Lumisden and J. Robertson, and sold at their Printing-house in the Fish-market," 1745, p. 10.

Torturing human sinners does not relieve the devils; in fact, it adds to their own torment. Notwithstanding, the malice of the devil is as steady as the flames. "No degree of misery though it be eternal will satisfy him so but that he would be glad to have it greater. How great is this cruelty and how great must all other wickedness be that is in proportion to it."[57]

Sinners in hell also torture themselves. Their pain is a "mixture of sorrow and rage."[58] Their lusts ever rage and there is never any satisfaction. In this world they gratified the sins by the nongratification of which they are tortured in hell.[59]

We know that many modern criminals dread fellow prisoners more than the prison itself and ostracism from the rest of society. They have more to fear from inmates than guards. This will not be true in hell. That is not because the inmates will not be cruel enough but because they cannot possibly be as cruel as their satanic guards who, so far from being restrained, are to do their damnedest. But even their worst tortures are gentleness by comparison with the real tormenter of hell, who is none other than God himself. There will be no comforts or consideration or "rights" from any direction—least of all from the one who sends these criminals to this dungeon. And they will not come out until they have paid the "uttermost farthing."

Edwards's famous sermon, *Sinners*,[60] had hearers hanging on to the pillars of the church and crying out for mercy. And this was merely a description of how God would deal with sinners and what he could do. The most terrifying preaching concerned what God is doing now in hell and will do forever. Edwards had said that no man could now see hell and live. It is a wonder that his people heard and lived. Edwards had written that the only way men can find peace is to deny the doctrine. It is not difficult to believe that Northampton sought peace by silencing the preacher of hell in 1750. I suspect that the "qualifications" controversy was the occasion; hell was the cause of the dismissal.

---

57. M690.
58. Matt. 13:47–50 (8), p. 1.
59. Luke 10:24, "That all the pleasure or comfort that ever wicked men are to have they have in this life" (p. 3), n.d.
60. *Op. cit.*

The Locality of Hell

"Tis probable that this earth after the conflagration shall be the place of the damned."

Even in their disembodied states, the wicked are taken at death to a local hell.

Departed spirits of wicked men are doubtless carried to some particular place in the universe, which God has prepared to be the receptacle of his wicked, rebellious, and miserable [subjects]; contrived a place of punishment; a place prepared on purpose to receive the filth of the creation and a place where the attributes of God's revenging justice shall be glorified; a place, the prison, where devils and wicked men are reserved till the day of judgment.[61]

From the same sermon it would appear that hell after the resurrection and day of judgment will be this world in conflagration. At least such would seem to be the implication of this description of the events following:

Immediately upon the finishing the judgment and the pronouncing that sentence will come the end of the world. Then the frame of this world shall be dissolved. The pronouncing of that sentence will probably be followed with amazing thunders that shall rend the heaven and shake the earth out of its place. II Pet. 3:10 . . . Then shall the sea and the waves roar and the rocks shall be thrown down and there shall be an universal wreck of this frame of the world. . . .[62]

This also is an expression of the wrath of God against sin. Then shall the heavens be dissolved and then the world shall be set on fire. As God in his wrath once destroyed the world by a flood of water so now shall he cause it to be all in a deluge of fire. And the heavens being on fire shall be dissolved and the elements shall melt with fervent heat. "And that great company of devils and wicked men must then enter into those everlasting burnings to which they are sentenced. . . ."[63] In *Miscellany* 275 Edwards

---

61. Rom. 2:8, 9, pp. 24, 25.
62. *Ibid.*, p. 38.
63. *Ibid.*, p. 39.

wrote: "'Tis probable that this earth after the conflagration shall be the place of the damned."

The arguments presented in the corresponding section on the locality of heaven apply here *mutatis mutandi*. For example, the resurrection of the body of the saints implies a place where they go, and this is paralleled by the fact of the resurrection of the bodies of the impenitent and where they must go. Again, man's natural condition as a body-soul being applies here. He continues to be a man even in hell and therefore would have a spatial body. Also, all the arguments that the fire must be literal imply that these bodies are in a definite locality. If the lost are to be punished in body as well as soul, there must be a location for this to be done. Edwards uses the word "prison," which would have to exist somewhere.[64]

Throughout our whole discussion of hell, implications for a locality will be obvious. To take but one example, the section dealing with hell's viewing of heaven is clearly corporeal as well as spiritual.

The Degrees of Torment

". . . the damned in hell would give the world to have the number of their sins one less."

Most people unfamiliar with the doctrine of hell would suppose that the nature of hell, as thus far described, is so frightful that any thought of gradations would be superfluous and impertinent, if not silly. Not so for Edwards, who devotes major space to these cantos of hell.

"The punishment and misery of wicked men in another world will be in proportion to the sin that they are guilty of."[65] The suffering for sins will be in relation to the heinousness and number of the sins and to the status of the sinner. The "second act of drunkenness . . . heats hell a great deal more than the first."

---

64. Cf. sermon on I Peter 3:19, 20 in Grosart, *Selections*, in which Edwards gives seven arguments for the fixity of that prison.
65. Matt. 5:22, fall 1727. Cf. M258.

Sinners who have lapsed from an awakened state will be punished more severely, but, most of all, leaders in sin aggravate their guilt.[66] "Such as these will doubtless be some of the lowest in hell—they will have the hottest place in the furnace.'"[67] Just as we punish ringleaders in crime most severely in this world, so too in the world to come.[68] The folly of augmenting future suffering by additional sins is driven home by the observation that we are not able to endure even an endless toothache, much less additional hell torments.[69]

Consequently, life in this world is the greatest punishment of all because its sinfulness leads to ever greater torment in hell. Thus the burden of the Romans 2:5 (1)[70] sermon: The sinner spends all his time here gathering fuel for his own fire there. Every continuance in sin adds to the heat of hell-fire. The longer sinners live, the more wrath they accumulate. Unlike worldly treasures these come easily and are never lost.[71] It would be far better for the unawakened to have spent the time in hell, than on earth; yea better for them to have spent ten thousand years in hell, instead of one on earth. "You will curse the day that you were born," Edwards warns the unawakened.[72] "Better were it for you if you met with nothing but sorrow and vexation in your ways. It would be better for you if your breath was taken from your nostrils, this day, and that you were nailed up in your coffin and that your soul should be amongst the damned this night.'"[73] In fact, "the damned in hell would be ready to give the world if they could to have the number of their sins to have been one less.'"[74]

The fact that hell has its degrees is part of the reason for Edwards's pathetic pleading with children not to start sinning early but to be converted and use their days in the joyous service

---

66. *Ibid.*, p. 4.
67. *Ibid.*, p. 24.
68. *Ibid.*
69. *Ibid.*, p. 25.
70. Rom. 2:5 (1), "Unawakened and impenitent sinners do heap up to themselves wrath against the day of wrath as men are wont to heap up treasures" (p. 4), Aug. 1731.
71. *Ibid.*
72. Rom. 1:24, "God sometimes punishes sin by giving men up to sin" (p. 3), fall 1734–winter 1726, p. 12.
73. *Ibid.*, pp. 11, 12.
74. Acts 8:20–22, "A man may eternally undo himself in one thought of his heart" (p. 3), June 1736, p. 25.

of their God.[75] If the best doctrine to present to sinners is hell, the best time is childhood. The number of special meetings for children that Edwards held, as well as the diligent attention he gave to the salvation of his own family, show his persuasion of this point. His approach to children was basically the same as the approach to their parents. They too were in danger of judgment and must learn to flee from the wrath that is to come upon them as well as upon older sinners. They were "young serpents" who had not yet learned to bite, but were full of poison.[76] They were no different in nature from their parents. They too were "children of the devil." Neither can they "bear hell among the devils," and they must beware of this dread judgment to which they are exposed. "Supposing, children," he exhorts, "you could now hear the cries of other wicked children that are gone to hell— Come therefore hearken to me—If you won't hearken but will go to hell . . ." (the sermon outline on Psalm 34:11 abruptly ends here).[77]

"Many persons," he warns the young people, "never get rid of the guilt of the sins of their youth, but it attends them to their graves and goes with them into eternity."[78] Youth is the best period in which to serve God, but, in spite of this fact, it is usually spent in vanity.[79] God will not excuse children nor does he forget their sins and the aggravation that they have sinned away the best time for their conversion. Young people often quench motions of the Holy Spirit and as a result never have them again all their lives, for God may be provoked to remove the Spirit in the beginning of their days. And even if God does not act so drastically, they put themselves under great and permanent spiritual disadvantages because the habits that they early contract are difficult to change. "Ill company" is a special snare in which the devil takes young people and carries them away for life.[80] And God never forgets.[81] After showing what young people are

---

75. Cf. chapter 4 in my *Steps to Salvation*.
76. Matt. 5:22, p. 6.
77. "Therefore now I would improve this Scripture to call upon you children now to forsake your sins and seek the fear of God" (p. 1). Private meeting of children, July 1741.
78. Job 20:11, to the young people at a private meeting, March 1733, Jan. 1756, p. 4.
79. *Ibid.*, pp. 4f.
80. *Ibid.*, p. 6.
81. *Ibid.*, p. 8.

missing, Edwards concludes: "So that you get nothing by spending your youth in sin, but are great losers for the present besides the danger that you incur of having your souls full of the sins of your youth when you die and then lying down with [them] in the grave and going with you to God's judgment seat and into eternity."[82]

Edwards used the death of young Billy Sheldon as the occasion for serious warning to the youth of his parish.[83] The boy died in the midst of the great awakening in February, 1740–41. He was cut off at such a time, the young people were told in a private meeting, to make you take full advantage of your opportunity. Very few of you, he continued, were more concerned for your souls than he was for his. He was not only deprived of further opportunity to seek salvation, but did not even have the use of his reason through much of his sickness. The exposition of the text is very brief, but the application is long and pleading: to exhort and beseech the young people "that are here present to get ready for death."[84] Edwards used the same sermon, with an altered application, for the funeral of his own daughter Jerusha at a later date.

Greater degrees of torment for great light spurned is the reason greater light can be a liability to all. "A man had better be a heathen than to differ from 'em only in common light and profession."[85] Some of the heathen, Edwards grants, "have been very moral and strict in their lives only that they have been heathen and have professed and practiced all the abominations of idolatry."[86] Unbelief and lusts are characteristic of the heathen, and Sodom and Gomorrah actually burned with hell-fire while on earth. Nevertheless, the lukewarm or merely nominal Christians' "guilt is much greater than that of the heathen because they sin under so much greater obligation to obedience."[87]

The definitive treatment on degrees of punishment is found in the sermon on Matthew 5:22, "That the punishment and misery of wicked men in another world will be in proportion to the sin

82. *Ibid.*, p. 19.
83. Job 14:2, "He cometh forth like a flower and is cut down," Feb. 1740–41; Feb. 21, 1747–48 ("on the occasion of the death of my daughter Jerusha").
84. *Ibid.*, p. 25.
85. Rev. 3:15, n.d., p. 2.
86. *Ibid.*, p. 3.
87. *Ibid.*, p. 23.

that they are guilty of.''[88] All men partake "equally" of original sin,[89] but men do not partake "equally" of "actual sins.''[90] The score is proportionately increased[91] in God's "debt book" although "he that commits one act of sin" (profanity, a breaking of the Sabbath, an intemperate act, etc.) "deserves capital punishment.'' He has merited only by one sinful act the eternal ruin of soul and body.[92] By a second act—assuming it was no worse— "he now deserves twice so hot a place in hell fire. . . .''[93] Heinousness of sins is next described and weighed,[94] aggravations considered,[95] and finally the influence or prestige of the sinner put into the balance.[96] It is no wonder that Edwards concludes that the sooner the persevering sinner dies the better—"if they go on in sin they had better die early than later.''[97] If they do go on it is better they be "moral" whether "they are converted or not.''[98] This doctrine makes fools of those who would enjoy this world since they expect to go to hell.[99] Those who are wise seek salvation even if they do not find it.[100] Otherwise, they will regret in hell that they had not sought salvation, though vainly.[101]

Growth in Misery

"After they have endured misery a thousand years they may have a more dreadful sense of an eternity of misery than they had at first."

Even in the sermon on "saints growing ripe for heaven" I suspected that I would find a clear statement on growing ripe for

---

88. Fall 1727, p. 4.
89. *Ibid.*, p. 5.
90. *Ibid.*, p. 4.
91. *Ibid.*
92. *Ibid.*
93. *Ibid.*, p. 5.
94. *Ibid.*, pp. 7, 8.
95. *Ibid.*, pp. 8-11.
96. *Ibid.*, pp. 11, 12.
97. *Ibid.*, p. 16.
98. *Ibid.*, p. 18.
99. *Ibid.*, p. 19.
100. *Ibid.*, p. 20.
101. *Ibid.*, p. 24.

hell. I was not disappointed. Although Edwards gave an excellent development of his doctrine (as we have seen above) in the application, we read:

> II. Let what has been said on this subject lead sinners to consider what *they* are ripening for. There are two kinds of persons that are here in this world in a preparatory state, elect and reprobates. Both are continued here in a state of preparation for an eternal state. Elect are here to be prepared [for heaven]. Reprobates are preparing [for hell]. They are ripening. And there are none [who] stand still, neither saints nor sinners.[102]

Then Edwards proceeds to a rather full outline of the way sinners grow into hell.[103]

So as sinners go on sinning they become more and more adapted to their new home—"more assimilated to the inhabitants of the infernal world."[104] They are already, in this world, sinking into the bottomless pit.

We have seen that sinners in hell suffer in varying degrees. Alas, even that particular degree seems to increase in hell itself. There the wicked continue to rebel against the just punishment of God, and that brings more just punishment. So growth in misery in hell seems as inevitable as growth in blessedness in heaven is certain. The devil, for example, seems to get some satisfaction in accomplishing some of his evil designs, but it hurts when he laughs. "I believe the devil has sometimes a kind of a pleasedness, when he accomplishes a design . . . [but] his pleasedness is but in order to his greater torment."[105]

The very realization of the wicked's plight makes their plight the sadder. By their rebellion against their misery they only intensify it. "Hell torments may increase this way, viz. as the damned may have more and more of a sense of eternity after they have endured misery a thousand years, they may have a more dreadful sense of an eternity of misery than they had at first."

Another thing that makes the ineffable pain of hell more painful is the envy and resentment of heaven's bliss. We will discuss

---

102. Rev. 14:15, "Subject—The saints growing ripe for heaven," Jan. 1743–44, p. 4.
103. *Ibid.*, pp. 42f.
104. *Ibid.*
105. M441.

this later. It is sufficient to note here that heaven's bliss adds to the burden of hell's present grief.

Finally, hell is masochistic. Why would anyone go there in the first place if he did not hate himself? Every sinner is in love with death. Edwards has often intoned that human dirge. Since hell changes nothing about the masochistic sinner he must go on destroying himself at an ever faster pace forever and forever. Edwards has observed that the devil is so incorrigibly malicious that hell's increasing torments do not deter him. The implication is that "natural men are God's enemies"[106] and become their own worst enemies. As men gather sticks in this world for their own fire they continue to do so even when they are actually engulfed in the flames!

Since M258 is relatively short and at the same time the fullest and most comprehensive reflection of Edwards on this somber point, we quote in full:

> *Hell.* I don't think we have good ground to be assured that the sins of damned spirits that they commit after their damnation are no way liable to punishment, because they ben't in a state of trial but in a state of punishment. However, I believe this in one sense is true and in another not. I believe all the misery, that ever they endure or shall endure to all eternity is a punishment of their sin while in a state of trial and every part of that misery a part of that punishment and all the deserved and justly due punishment of that sin. So that those that have sinned most in a state of trial shall be punished most to all eternity and in an exact proportion. And yet it shall be so ordered by the wisdom of God that various parts of their punishment shall be so timed and placed and circumstanced as to be punishment also of their several acts of pride, of malice, and spite against God and against his creatures that are not in a state of punishment. Thus God brings the punishment of the devils upon 'em for their proud rebellion in heaven in this way by making them the cause of their own vexation and torment to all eternity by their continually renewed acts of pride and spite. He gives them over forever to that same disposition which they exercised when they fell and by that means makes them forever a-procuring their own misery. And this is a misery they are plunged into as a punishment of their first rebellion. Tis certain by the word of God that the devils are thus punished. They are punished for their procuring the fall of mankind. God curses the serpent for it, and,

---

106. Rom. 5:10 (two sermons), Aug. 1736, p. 4.

without doubt, God, in that curse, had a principal reference to the devil, who is the old serpent; the seed of the woman breaking his head is in punishment for that act of his. By means of Christ the Redeemer, God renders all Satan's incessant labours and endeavours for the overthrow of mankind and for defeating God's design of glorifying himself in them, a means of his own confusion and vexation and of abundantly more brightly manifesting the glory of God and advancing the happiness of the elect. He is a means of one of mankind being his Judge, and so the event of his own great endeavours will prove every way exceeding contradiction and mortification of his own restless, proud, malicious, and revengeful spirit.

Hell Beholding This World

"Wicked men in hell will remember how things were with them here in this world."

Edwards has a couplet of unpublished sermons which concern the theme of this and the next section. Luke 16:25 (1) develops this doctrine: "Wicked men in hell will remember how things were with them here in this world."[107] The second in the little series on this text taught that "the wicked in hell will be sensible what a happy state the saints are in in heaven."[108] We will first consider nostalgia in hell.

This parable of Dives and Lazarus, though not to be taken literally ("we need not suppose that there ever was actually such a conversation"),[109] justifies the doctrine that hell remembers this world. The lost "remember what good things they enjoyed here in this world."[110] While they enjoyed the good things, they "felt nothing of the fiery wrath of God."[111] Now it is the reverse. They will remember the "bottle of liquor," "friends," "comfortable habitation," and how they were "a great deal better off than many of the godly."[112] Of particular poignancy will be their

---

107. N.d., Sept. 1757, p. 3.
108. N.d., p. 2.
109. Luke 16:25 (1), p. 3.
110. *Ibid.*, p. 4.
111. *Ibid.*
112. *Ibid.*, p. 6.

recollection of "opportunities" and means they had for obtaining salvation[113] when "God waited to be gracious unto them."[114] They remember how they were warned "that if once they got into hell they should never get out."[115] Especially, they will remember their sins,[116] including thinking that hell was a mere "dream."[117]

"It will make their sufferings the more heavy and sinking to think how things were with them in this world."[118] So Edwards continues throughout the application. "How dreadful will it be to 'em to consider..."[119] "And how will it aggravate..."[120] "How will it torment 'em to think of..."[121] Among other tortures hell will be the place of the eternal "I told you so."

It is interesting that Edwards does not, in this sermon, reflect on Dives's apparent compassion for his brother (still sinning in this world) and desire that he not make Dives's fatal mistake (an interest in the Kingdom of God on the part of lost Dives?)

Edwards often studies the remorse which sinners feel when they look back upon their lives in this world. (We have seen that sorrow as well as rage make up their pain.) "Vicious persons when once they come to taste the bitter fruits of their evil courses, will greatly lament their folly in not hearkening to the counsels and warnings that were given them."[122] Again, "convictions are terrible when they come too late for repentance."[123] In a third sermon on the same text: "when wicked men come to hell they will believe what they heard in the preaching of the word.... They will see what fools they were."[124]

"You'll curse and blaspheme" in hell, preached Edwards, and also "curse yourself" because "it will be terrible to be aware that you have been the cause of your own destruction)... to know that

113. *Ibid.*, p. 7.
114. *Ibid.*
115. *Ibid.*
116. *Ibid.*, pp. 8-10.
117. *Ibid.*, p. 10.
118. *Ibid.*, p. 11.
119. *Ibid.*, p. 12.
120. *Ibid.*, p. 13.
121. *Ibid.*
122. Prov. 5:11-13 (1), before 1733, p. 2.
123. Prov. 5:11-13 (2), Oct. 1741, p. 2.
124. (3) Feb. 1752, St. Ind., Moh. (Andover Collection), p. 1.

you have undone yourself by your own folly and to know that tis too late to correct your errour."[125]

In other words, it is remembering the folly committed in this world that heightens the suffering for it in the next.

Hell Beholding Heaven

"The songs of the blessed will give them a more clear sense of the greatness of their own misery."

We have noted that the sermons on Luke 16:25 deal with the wicked in hell remembering how things were with them in this world and being "sensible what a happy state the saints are in in heaven."[126] We have noted the first sermon. Now, the second.

Edwards seems to think this text is a counterpart of Revelation 18:20, on which he preached the famous sermon we have mentioned in which the saints in glory are made happy as they see the smoke of hell ascend. Here, the rich man is represented as seeing Lazarus the wretched beggar "comforted" in Abraham's bosom while "thou art tormented."[127] Not only will the "goats" see the "sheep" on Christ's right hand at the day of judgment, but "the Scriptures seem to speak as though the world of misery would be in sight of the world of happiness" (Isa. 66:24),[128] though it is "far off and though there was a great gulf fixed between."[129] "Though they see the majesty and greatness of God and that the saints are happy in heaven, they can never understand what it is that gives them pleasure."[130] They will have "no relish for any such kind of happiness."[131] If admitted to heaven, they "would be out of their element."[132]

---

125. Prov. 5:11–13 (2), "Convictions are terrible when they come too late for repentance" (p. 2), Oct. 1741, pp. 20, 21.
126. Sermon (2), n.d., p. 2.
127. *Ibid.*, p. 1.
128. *Ibid.*, pp. 3, 4.
129. *Ibid.*, p. 4.
130. *Ibid.*, p. 5.
131. *Ibid.*
132. *Ibid.*, p. 6.

Yet they will know enough to be miserable. "How will you
bear to hear them singing for joy of heart, when your work day
and night will be nothing but to cry for sorrow of heart and
howl—"133

The two-way formula that applies to hell contemplating heaven
as well as heaven contemplating hell is succinctly stated. ". . . we
have a more lively apprehension of any good we enjoy by comparing it with the contrary evil, so on the other hand, we have a
more sensible apprehension of any evil that we suffer by our
seeing the contrary good."134 The greatest sting for the wicked
will be realizing that all this loss and all this pain was "through
their own sottish negligence, and because they would not do what
they could do."135

Edwards takes this theme from the beginning of the Luke
13:28f. sermon. "Wicked men will hereafter have this to aggravate their woe that they shall see many of all kinds and nations
admitted into glory when they themselves are thrust out."136 The
very outline shows the building up to this climax:

Proposition 1: "Wicked men shall see others admitted into
glory"
Proposition 2: "They shall see many of all sorts and
nations. . . ."
Proposition 3: "This shall be when they themselves are thrust
out"
Proposition 4: "This will aggravate their grief and woe."137

Edwards is not certain of the exact location at the confrontation
but only that the two parties will see each other.

We know not how far the two worlds, the world of happiness and
the world of misery, may be within each other's view. It seems as
though the glorified in heaven should some way or other have an
apprehension of the damned in hell and also the damned an apprehension of the glory of the saints in heaven as though they had
a view of each other's state.138

133. *Ibid.*, p. 13.
134. *Ibid.*, p. 15.
135. *Ibid.*, p. 16.
136. N.d., "This I have preached at New Place and at Stockbridge to Indians," p. 3.
137. *Ibid.*, p. 3.
138. *Ibid.*, pp. 3, 4.

He cites Revelation 14:10 and the parable of Dives and Lazarus in support. However all this may be, Edwards is certain that at the day of judgment "the wicked shall see others glorified."[139] They will see them mount up to meet the Lord in the air, be received, seated at his right hand, and crowned. "Those things will be transacted most publicly in open sight of all wicked men."[140] The lost will see the redeemed "floating to Christ from every region of the earth"—among them those whom the wicked had despised in this world.[141]

Apparently all this will only surprise the sinful spectators who are still expecting to join the universal throng. But when they try to enter they are "thrust out." When they "strive" to enter (because they recognize Abraham and others they thought to be their friends) they are "thrust back violently."[142] The grim fact settles in and becomes ever grimmer as they continue to behold the contrasting felicity of the heavenly company—"seeing of their blessedness will give them a more lively sense of the greatness of their own misery."[143] As the hallelujahs continue, "the songs of the blessed will make their wailing and moans the louder and more bitter."[144]

Our most comprehensive Edwardsean sermonic survey, Romans 2:8, 9 (which together with 2:10 constitutes a veritable Baedecker of heaven and hell), shows that this "aggravation" goes on forever. This sermon mentions only briefly that while the sins of the wicked are being exposed at the day of judgment, "then shall they stand at the left hand in these circumstances while they see others that they have known sitting at the right hand of Christ in glory."[145] Then "will be the most dreadful . . . words to them that ever were heard" (their sentence).[146] It will be "aggravated by their hearing of the blessed sentence pronounced on those that shall be at the right."[147]

---

139. *Ibid.*, p. 4.
140. *Ibid.*, p. 5.
141. *Ibid.*, p. 6.
142. *Ibid.*, p. 8.
143. *Ibid.*, p. 10.
144. *Ibid.*, p. 14.
145. Rom. 2:8, 9, p. 36.
146. *Ibid.*
147. *Ibid.*, p. 37.

The Eternality of Hell

". . . as sure as God is true there will absolutely be no end to the misery of hell."

"The torments of hell will be eternal"[148] is the title of the most complete couplet of sermons Edwards ever preached on this subject. Endlessness is the aspect of hell that most "prevents peace." There is nothing that so "damps the pleasures of the ungodly."[149] Consequently, men's theories oppose it. "Eternity is the sting of the doctrine of hell torments whereby chiefly it is that it stings the consciences of wicked men and there is no other way to avoid the torment of it but to deny it."[150] Edwards will "clear up" the meaning of eternality, though he reminds us that "the infinite cannot be perfectly comprehended by that which is finite."[151]

We have no positive idea of the eternality of hell. "It is that duration that has no end."[152] Since Edwards cannot define, he lists some of eternity's properties, negatively and positively. Negatively: first, it cannot be divided into integral parts;[153] there is no half of eternity. Second, it cannot be distinguished by periods, such as youth or old age. Third, a great period has no more proportion to it than a short one; a thousand ages is as much less as a minute.[154] Fourth, the eternality of hell cannot be made more or less by addition or subtraction.[155] Fifth, it will be forever only beginning. "The wicked after they have suffered many millions of ages, will be as it were, . . . only setting out in torment."[156]

"Eternal" means that there will be "no end."[157] Then follows Edwards's attack on annihilation which we will develop below.

---

148. Mark 9:44, winter-summer 1730, p. 3. Cf. also the very full discussion in *Remarks on Important Theological Controversies,* "Concerning the Endless Punishment of those who die Impenitent," Hickman, II, 515-25.
149. *Ibid.*
150. *Ibid.,* p. 4.
151. *Ibid.,* p. 5.
152. *Ibid.*
153. *Ibid.,* p. 7.
154. *Ibid.,* p. 9.
155. *Ibid.,* pp. 9, 10.
156. *Ibid.,* p. 10.
157. *Ibid.,* pp. 10f.

Not only will there be no annihilation, but not even "altera-
tion."[158] God's veracity is at stake.[159] After this survey of scrip-
tural doctrine Edwards concludes that "except God's word passes
away and falls to the ground we may be assured that the torments
of hell will be eternal."[160]

The major part of the second sermon on Mark 9:44 is concerned with why hell's torments are eternal. For one thing, those
in hell "deserve it."[161] Secondly, God has many good ends in the
endlessness of punishment,[162] such as the glorification of his
majesty, his justice, and his grace. And lastly the sight of hell
torments will make the happiness of saints greater.[163]

Perhaps, Edwards's deepest cry to his age was: "This doctrine
is indeed awful and dreadful. It is dreadful to think of it, but yet
tis what God the eternal God who made us and who has us soul
and body in his hands has abundantly declared unto us, so that so
sure as God is true there will absolutely be no end to the misery
of hell."[164] Such express and deliberate "reasoned reflections" on
the quantitative endlessness of hell makes the following comment
of Haroutunian puzzling, to say the least. He supposes that this
punishment is infinite more in quality than in duration.

> Edwards, in his appeals to the wicked of the day, however, falls
> back upon descriptions of the "future life" which are commensu-
> rate with the minds of his audiences; and one is irresistibly led to
> believe that he was thoroughly sincere in these popular presen-
> tations, *in spite of his more reasoned reflections* on time and
> eternity.[165]

This is bowdlerizing Edwards's theology. It may well be the
besetting sin of this century as was bowdlerizing his style in the
nineteenth century—a classic case of straining the gnat and swal-
lowing the camel.

In still more "reasoned reflections on time and eternity," Ed-

---

158. *Ibid.*, pp. 17f.
159. *Ibid.*, pp. 19f.
160. *Ibid.*, p. 23.
161. *Ibid.*
162. *Ibid.*, pp. 24–26.
163. *Ibid.*, p. 26.
164. *Ibid.*, p. 12.
165. *Piety Versus Moralism*, p. 133 (italics ours).

wards argues from Matthew 25:46[166] for the endlessness of hell. The expressions used in that context for eternal things are also used for perdition. They are the same words used for eternal happiness (which concept is never questioned). The "uttermost farthing" of Matthew 5:26 and the absoluteness of Mark 9:44 are again cited in evidence of the eternity of hell's torments.

Furthermore, Edwards annihilates annihilation. The wicked in the world to come will beg for annihilation, but Edwards will not allow this hope. He destroys it with a battery of arguments. First, the Bible teaches eternal punishment.[167] It is eternal, for the very word used for eternal life is used for eternal death. And this punishment implies pain, which annihilation is not. Annihilation is the relief which the wicked, begging for, will never receive. As the sermon on Revelation 6:15,16 poignantly describes, "Wicked men will hereafter earnestly wish to be turned to nothing and forever cease to be that they may escape the wrath of God."[168] Second, it is also clear that the wicked "shall be sensible of the punishment they are under."[169] Third, degrees of punishment preclude annihilation.[170] Fourth, "the Scripture is very express and abundant in this matter that the eternal punishment is in sensible misery and torment and not annihilation."[171] Furthermore, annihilation is no state at all and is therefore inconsistent with man's soul, which is never destroyed.[172] Sixth, men would never know their judgment if annihilation were their punishment. Instead of God repaying them face to face they would never have to face God at all.[173] But, in the seventh place, wicked men are still alive in hell now, fearing the resurrection of their bodies,[174] as the devils are now dreading the further punishment which is awaiting them. Again, it could not be said that it was better for the wicked not to have been born if they have

---

166. "The misery of the wicked in hell will be absolutely eternal," p. 2, April 1739. Hickman, II, 83f.

167. *Ibid.*, p. 12.

168. Aug. 1731–Dec. 1732, Oct. 1755, p. 4.

169. Matt. 25:46, April 1739, p. 12.

170. *Ibid.*, p. 14.

171. *Ibid.*, pp. 14f.

172. Matt. 7:13 (2), "I would show what kind of destruction that is that is spoken of in the text," Nov. 1744 (pp. 2, 3).

173. Matt. 25:46, p. 13.

174. Rom. 2:8, 9.

no judgment awaiting them.[175] (In fact, the righteous generally suffer more in this world than the wicked, which would make the latter's annihilation unfair.) Ninth, what is the meaning of a burning furnace heated to different degrees if none were ever to be cast into it?[176] Moreover, if the judgment of God begins in the house of God it surely will not spare the unrighteous, and if it was done in a green tree (the innocent Christ) what will happen to the dry?[177] Finally, how could Christ have had to die for us when no punishment threatened?[178]

A kind of empirical argument for eternality is also found. Sinners after death will continue to hate God, as we have seen, and will, therefore, continue endlessly to incur his wrath. If it was imagined that human guilt was only finite, men would sin endlessly in hell, and that would bring endless pains, anyway.[179] If one asked whether men would not stop sinning when they saw, in hell, the immediate and inescapable punishment that followed, we assume that Edwards would say they would not and could not stop. Their nature being unchanged, they would never cease sinning in hell any more than in this world. Punishment never prevents sin but only the expression of it. In hell nothing is gained, as here, by curbing expression. There is no hope of salvation or use in "seeking" it. But, we persist, could it not be argued that lost souls would see an advantage in less expression of malice and therefore, while hating God still, express it less and thereby prevent hell from becoming more hellish? No, ineradicable malice would always increase with exercise. And, it may be so great as to be incapable of non-expression, as is the case with the devils, who do actually find some "pleasedness" in the accomplishments of their malice. At least their malice continues "even in the midst of extreme pain."

That raises another problem with which Edwards wrestles. Are men punished for their sins committed in a state of punishment as well as in a state of trial? His answer is yes and no. Punishment is based on the trial period, but "if we should suppose that the

---

175. Matt. 25:46, *passim.*
176. Mark 9:44.
177. *Ibid.* Cf. M280; Rom. 2:8, 9, p. 24.
178. Matt. 25:46. Cf. below.
179. M574.

punishment that the sins of this life deserve is but finite; that it deserves only temporary misery, yet while they are suffering that they continue sinning still and so contract a new debt, and again while they are paying that they contract another, and so *in infinitum.*"[180]

Ultimately, the eternality of hell is based on the nature of God. If God is the inflictor of hell's tortures and his word, nature, justice, and wrath are eternal and immutable, hell must be eternal. "God," Edwards tells us, "will never weary." The sermon on Matthew 24:35 has this theme: "That God never fails of his word."[181] The main burden of this message is the assurance to God's people that he fulfills his promises. Nevertheless, it is also true that God's Word also includes threats, and he is just as faithful to them as he is to his promises. God threatens that hell is eternal. Therefore

> there is no room for any secret hope that after they have lain in the flames for a great many ages that God will be satisfied with their punishment and take pity upon 'em and so release 'em. God won't be any more inclined to pity them after they have lain there millions of ages than he will the first moment. . . . God's Word that cannot pass away is engaged to make them miserable to all eternity.[182]

The very climax of *Sinners in the Hands of an Angry God* is that the awful wrath to which sinners are now exposed in the hands of an angry God is that, "'tis everlasting wrath."[183] It would be dreadful to suffer the fierceness and the wrath of almighty God one moment; but some must suffer it to all eternity.

> When you look forward, you shall see a long forever, a boundless duration before you, which will swallow up your thoughts, and amaze your soul; and you will absolutely despair of ever having any deliverance, any end, any mitigation, any rest at all; you will know certainly that you must wear out long ages, millions of millions of ages, in wrestling and conflicting with this almighty merciless vengeance; and then when you have so done, when so

---

180. *Ibid.*
181. N.d., p. 3.
182. *Ibid.*, p. 9.
183. *Op. cit.*

many ages have actually been spent by you in this manner, you will know that all is but a point to what remains. So that your punishment will indeed be infinite. Oh who can express what the state of a soul in such circumstances is! All that we can possibly say about it, gives but a very feeble, faint representation of it; tis inexpressible and inconceivable. For, *who knows the power of God's anger?*[184]

Probably nowhere does Edwards face up more feelingly to the problem of hell and the nature of God than in the sermon on Revelation 19:2, "Tis not inconsistent with the attributes of God to punish ungodly men with a misery that is eternal."[185] In a massive understatement he says that men find it difficult to reconcile endless punishment with those perfections which the Scripture attributes to God, such as his being most just and righteous and also merciful. Men picture God as a God of great tenderness and compassion who is far from being cruel; He is love itself and is not willing that any should perish. Men cannot conceive how it should be consistent with the nature of such a God to make a creature so extremely miserable perpetually, without a moment's rest, and to continue to inflict such torments forever. But God will make them wear out the visible world. When the sun is grown old and the heavens wax old as a garment, still God will not abate at all their misery. Edwards, as he describes the feelings of the profane, seems almost to sympathize with the "wicked with their blasphemous thought."

After pages of this he comes to the solemn, crushing conclusion that however dreadful the punishment be and however terrible to think of it, yet if it is no more than proportionate to the crime, it is just. "If the crime and punishment do but keep a proportion then justice is safe; let the punishment go never so far." Therefore if there is such a thing as an infinitely heinous crime, it will follow that the punishment may be infinitely dreadful. Though that infinite punishment be amazing to think of, that is no argument against justice. He then proceeds to show that sin against God is, indeed, infinitely heinous.

---

184. *Op. cit.*, p. 21.
185. N.d., p. 4.

The Rationale of Hell

("Sin against God in God's idea is infinite, and the punishment is infinite.")

The basic proof for hell is the Bible. We have shown in our "Jonathan Edwards and the Bible"[186] how he argues that it is rational to believe that the Bible is the revelation of God. We need not re-examine the biblical evidence that hell is true since it is a part of our entire discussion above and below. Edwards also argued rationally that if there is a God he would reveal himself and that the Bible is the only such revelation. Likewise, if God intended to judge the world he would reveal that fact and so the Bible does.

The rationalization for hell is in terms of harmony or proportion. "According to thy fear (terribleness) so is thy wrath."[187] Because of this proportion the suffering of offenders must be infinite as is the majesty of the offended one. Even present suffering is in proportion to the manifestation of the divine majesty.

> . . . As God's favour is infinitely desireable so tis a part of his infinite awful majesty that his displeasure is infinitely dreadful which it would not be if it were contrary to the perfection of his nature to punish eternally. If God's majesty were not infinite and his displeasure were not infinitely dreadful he would be less glorious.[188]

An offense against an infinite being is greater than any finite degree of badness and is therefore an infinite degree of badness.[189] If one adds greatness to a being he adds greatness to an offense against him. Thus he adds infinite badness since the offense is against an infinite being.

Here a criticism arises: a finite person does not have a complete idea of the infinite excellence and therefore cannot be guilty of infinite offense. Edwards answers that "eternal punishment is

---

186. *Tenth: An Evangelical Quarterly* 9, 4 (October, 1979), 2–71.
187. Ps. 90:11.
188. Mnn stresses the infinite dement of sin.
189. Mnn.

just in the same respects infinite as the crime, and in no other.'' So, the crime is infinite though not in the one committing it; and the punishment is accordingly administered: "it is itself infinite, but is never suffered infinitely. Indeed if the soul was capable of having at once a full and complete idea of the eternity of misery, then it would properly be infinite suffering." The soul being incapable of this, ["eternity is suffered as an infinite God is offended, that is, according to the comprehension of the mind. . . . Sin against God in God's idea is infinite, and the punishment is infinite no otherwise but in the idea of God. . . ."[190]

There are rational arguments for hell as well.[191] Some lie in plain view—namely, the pain and suffering of men in this present world. This itself shows that God is "not averse to have them suffer." If God were, Edwards seems to be supposing, he would not have so ordained. He could have prevented suffering and he could terminate it, if he pleased. Empirical facts settle one point indisputably: God and creature-pain are not mutually exclusive. The usual form of the problem of evil (evil proves that God is either not omnipotent or not good) is false. God is omnipotently good and he ordains evil. It is therefore good that there should be evil. This theodicy is a foundation for the possibility of hell, which, when justice and wisdom are added, becomes the necessity for hell.

That brings us to the argument for hell from moral government. "Wicked men have no reason to doubt the truth of anything that is said in the word of God, concerning the future punishment of the ungodly, or to suspect whether it be true."[192] God made this world and must regulate it, as a moral creator would, according to some rule by which it must ultimately be judged and sentenced.[193]

---

190. M44.
191. For example, somewhere Edwards observes that if one man's sin could bring ruin to the whole world it is not inconceivable that a man's sin could ruin himself eternally. Cf. also M572. Also in the sermon on Exod. 9:12-16 (3) Edwards uses such expressions as "not inconceivable," "certainly true," "rational."
192. The conclusion of the sermon lecture on Rom. 1:20 ("The being and attributes of God are clearly to be seen by the works of creation" (p. 1) (June 1743, Aug. 1756) is interesting because it follows Edwards's fullest rational demonstration of the existence of God and warns sinners that there is no rational foundation for their hoping to escape the eternal wrath threatened in the Bible.
193. Hickman, II, 485f.

While Edwards does not usually populate hell with named individuals, as Dante does, he is quite specific about Antiochus Epiphanes, who persecuted the Jewish church in the intertestamental period. Acting apparently on his own moral inclinations, Edwards would not have wanted Antiochus ever to be delivered from his endless, indescribable tortures of body and soul because of what he did to the bodies of men. Some of the brutal Roman Catholic persecutors seemed to Edwards to deserve endless suffering: "the extremity of hell torments don't seem too much for them." [194] He defends himself: it is our insensitivity to sin that prevents our realizing how hell-deserving sin is. Our "devilish dispositions" make sin not appear "horrid." Is Edwards speaking for himself? Does he really think and feel in his own heart that Antiochus and certain popes should endlessly suffer for sins that ended long ago, or is he unconsciously returning to his role as defender of the ways of God? We think that for Edwards these were one and the same.

If a righteous God must punish wicked men, Edwards argues, this punishment must be eternal. Sin, he says, is enmity against the giver of all being. It is rational to suppose that this would incur the hatred of this great Being, and this Being's hatred and wrath would be as infinite as he is. The sermon on Romans 3:19 enters somewhat thoroughly into this difficult theme. We will summarize this preachment because it catches up in one statement virtually all the lines of Edwards's reasoning that show the necessity of eternal punishment.

Sereno Dwight wrote that the discourses that, beyond any others Edwards preached, had an immediate saving effect were several from Romans 3:19.

> The sermon . . . literally stops the mouth of every reader, and compels him, as he stands before his Judge, to admit, if he does not feel, the justice of his sentence. I know not where to find, in any language, a discourse so well adapted to strip the impenitent sinner of every excuse, to convince him of his guilt, and to bring him low before the justice and holiness of God. According to the estimate of Mr. Edwards, it was far the most powerful and effec-

---

194. M527. "When I read some instances of the monstrous and amazing cruelty of some popish persecutors, I have such a sense of the horridness of what they did that the extremity of hell torments don't seem too much for them."

tual of his discourses, and we scarcely know of any other sermon which has been favoured with equal success.[195]

This is the only sermon on Romans which was published in Edwards's lifetime[196] (apart from those on Romans 4:5, which were, however, printed as the treatise on *Justification by Faith*). Its popular title is "The Justice of God in the Damnation of Sinners." Edwards's actual doctrine is: "'Tis just with God eternally to cast off, and destroy sinners."[197]

The sermon begins with a review of the first part of the Epistle to the Romans. Edwards reminds us that his text was written to show that all men, Gentiles and Jews alike, stood condemned. The words of 3:19 sum it all up: "That every mouth may be stopped." He moves to his doctrine which he develops by two considerations: man's sinfulness and God's sovereignty.

First, the "infinitely evil nature of all sin" is shown. This is argued by saying that "a crime is more or less heinous, according as we are under greater or lesser obligations to the contrary,"[198] and the preacher maintains that "our obligation to love, honour, and obey any being, is in proportion to his loveliness, honourableness, and authority."[199] From this it is quickly apparent that there is an infinite obligation to obey God and that disobedience is infinitely heinous and, if infinitely heinous, deserves infinite punishment. In answer to an objection against such punishment on the ground of the certainty of sin, Edwards presents a principle that is a major thesis in his great work on *The Freedom of the Will:* "The light of nature teaches all mankind, that when an injury is voluntary, it is faulty, without any manner of consideration of what there might be previously to determine the futurition of that evil act of the will."[200]

The sovereignty of God in the punishment of sinners is considered next.[201] First, God's sovereignty relieved God of any obliga-

195. Dwight, I, 141, 142.
196. *Dissertation on Various Important Subjects* (Boston; printed and sold by S. Kneeland and T. Green, 1738), pp. 192f.
197. *Ibid.,* p. 195.
198. *Ibid.,* p. 196.
199. *Ibid.,* p. 197.
200. *Ibid.,* p. 199.
201. *Ibid.,* pp. 201f.

tion to keep men from sinning[202] in the first creation. Second, it was also God's right to determine whether every man should be tried individually or by a representative.[203] After the Fall, God had a sovereign right to redeem or not to redeem, and to redeem whom he pleased if he pleased.[204] The rest of the sermon, approximately three times the length of the development, is given over to a probing application which, it is not surprising, found many out. Much of it is an unfolding of the doctrine that "'tis just with God eternally to cast off and destroy you.'"[205] After showing how proper it would be for God to destroy them since they have despised his mercy, ("there is something peculiarly heinous in sin against the mercy of God more than his other attributes"),[206] he also accuses them of being unwilling to come even if they could.[207] Edwards ends pastorally with great encouragement to the redeemed, arguing that it was a much greater thing that Christ died than that all the world should burn in hell.[208]

If this is the rationale for hell, hell is the rationale for much of Edwards's preaching, in spite of its appearing imprecatory. Speaking of the imprecations of the Bible, he observes:

> We cannot think that those imprecations we find in the Psalms and Prophets, were out of their own hearts; for cursing is spoken of as a very dreadful sin in the Old Testament; and David, whom we hear oftener than any other praying for vengeance on his enemies, by the history of his life, was of a spirit very remote from spiteful and revengeful. . . . And some of the most terrible imprecations that we find in all the Old Testament, are in the New spoken of as prophetical, even those in the 109th Psalm; as in Acts 1:20. . . . They wish them ill, not as personal, but as public enemies to the church of God.

Apparently, therefore, although Edwards regarded himself as the spokesman of God in these sermons, he was still issuing warnings, in God's name, of what would happen to the impenitent. He was not himself invoking judgment or issuing anathemas.

---

202. *Ibid.*, p. 201.
203. *Ibid.*, p. 203.
204. *Ibid.*, pp. 203, 204.
205. *Ibid.*, pp. 204–43.
206. *Ibid.*, p. 218.
207. *Ibid.*, pp. 223f.
208. *Ibid.*, p. 241.

As a matter of fact, all the evidence tends to indicate that his fervent preaching of hell stemmed hardly more from his obedience to God than from his deep love to mankind. Believing in the reality of hell for the sinner, what would a benevolent man do but everything in his power to warn against such an awful retribution? Some of the exhortations of Edwards are the most drawn-out, pathetic appeals to the unconverted that can be found in the history of the Christian pulpit. This is not the spirit of sadism. Ironically, if Edwards, believing as he did, had been a sadist, he would never have said a word about perdition.

If it be granted that Edwards preached these minatory sermons because he believed that God appointed his preachers to warn men about perdition, we would still expect him to probe the purpose of God in this. And indeed he has much to say about the strategy of preaching perdition. In a word, his reasoning appears to be: hell is about all of spiritual reality that can affect most unconverted men. Self-interest, their motivating principle, would concern them to avoid such a doom. Natural men cannot see God's excellency, but they can hear his thunders. One is reminded of a character in a Hemingway novel being asked if he ever thought of God and answering that he did sometimes when wakened in the middle of the night by a thunderstorm.

> Most wicked men that have heard of hell have these internal uneasinesses, arising from the thoughts of their unsafeness. . . . They don't manifest it outwardly. . . . Though other men cannot perceive it yet he himself feels it. . . . The most bold, and daring of sinners, are the most fearful and timorous upon a death-bed. How do they fear and tremble. How do they shrink back. How do their proud hearts tremble at the sight of his ghastly visage.[209]

On the other hand, a principal means of being lost is thinking that there will be no punishment.[210]

Many of Edwards's sermons illustrate his use of this doctrine in evangelistic preaching. The sermon on Jude 13 (1) is an example: "The wicked in another world shall eternally be overwhelmed with the most dismal and perfect gloominess of mind."[211] This theme is followed by a searching application,

---

209. Prov. 29:25, "They are safe that trust in God" (p. 2), before 1733, p. 12.
210. *Ibid.,* pp. 12–14.
211. Jan. 1748–49, p. 2.

after which the preacher has his people asking, "What shall we do?" His answer is "You must be born again."[212] Unlike most modern evangelists, who would either let the matter rest once they had advised men to be born again or would assure them, in Arminian fashion, that they would be born again if they would believe, Edwards tells his hearers to repair to God for the sovereign gift of the new birth. "In order to that [new birth] you must seek it in the first place."[213] Our evangelist does not believe that faith is a potentiality of corrupt natures. Until God gives the disposition to believe, men remain unbelieving. There is, therefore, nothing that men can do to produce regeneration. But they can seek God (and Edwards always encourages them) in order that God may, if it is his sovereign pleasure, bestow this gift upon them.

On other occasions, Edwards does not proceed from the fear of hell to the topic of the new birth. Rather, he sometimes dilates on the necessity of fleeing the wrath that is to come. Of course, there is only one main end in fleeing, and that is being born again. But in some sermons the preacher is intent merely on having his people flee. No doubt they understood what was involved in fleeing and why they were advised to do it.

To those who protested against Edwards's preaching in his own day he vindicated his "scare theology" in the following manner:

> Some talk of it as an unreasonable thing to fright persons to heaven, but I think it is a reasonable thing to endeavour to fright persons away from hell. They stand upon its brink, and are just ready to fall into it, and are senseless of their danger. Is it not a reasonable thing to fright a person out of a house on fire?[214]

Edwards never entertained the notion that anyone could be scared into heaven (but only into thinking about it and "seeking" for it). Constantly he speaks as in the sermon on Job 14:5: "There is no promise in the whole Word of God that prayings and cries that arise merely from fear and an expectation of punishment

212. *Ibid.*, p. 17.
213. *Ibid.*
214. Cf. *Steps to Salvation* (Philadelphia: Westminster Press, 1960), chapter 3, pp. 24–34. Hos. 5:15 (1), "That tis God's manner to make men sensible of their misery and unworthiness before he appears in his mercy and love to them," n.d., Hickman, II, 830f.

shall be heard especially if they have been willfully negligent till then."[215] He goes further in the sermon on Luke 16:31, "Scripture Warnings Best Adapted to the Conversion of Sinners,"[216] by pointing out that sinners are not scared into heaven but that total fear would make them all the more the children of hell. This is the reason he does not believe it would be salutary for men to have a preview of actual hell, as awakening as that might appear to be: "It would make them more like devils; and set them a blaspheming as the damned do. For while the hearts of men are filled with natural darkness, they cannot see the glory of the divine justice appearing in such extreme torments."[217]

This remark about the inadvisability of showing a sinner the actual hell, reveals, incidentally, that Edwards sought to avoid engendering a wrong kind of fear. The sermon on Jeremiah 5:21–22 affords a good discussion of the two varieties of fear. The doctrine is that "'tis a sottish and unreasonable thing for men not to fear God and tremble at his presence."[218] In the course of defining what this fear is, Edwards finds occasion to reflect that "those that have a sinful fear of God fear God as evil, but a right fear fears him as great and excellent."[219] Thus there is a right and wrong fear of God. This wrong fear of God, fearing him as an evil and dreadful being, drives men from God. "A sinful fear makes men afraid to come to God."[220]

But, on the other hand, there is a proper fear of God, as the good and holy being that he is, and this right fear makes men afraid to go from him. If men fear God as they fear the devil, they flee from him, but if they fear him as the being he really is, they will flee to him. It is this wrong fear or "servile fear" which is cast out by love. But love does not cast out this dread of displeasing and offending God, for this holy fear does not only dread the fruits of God's displeasure but the displeasure itself.

Putting the picture together, we get this Edwardsean rationale

215. Job 14:5, "That God unalterably determines the limits of every man's life" (p. 2), n.d., p. 15.

216. Luke 16:31, "The warnings of God's Word are more fitted to obtain the ends of awakening sinners, and bringing them to repentance, than the rising of one from the dead to warn them," n.d., Hickman, II, 68.

217. *Ibid.*, p. 70.

218. March 1738, p. 5.

219. *Ibid.*, pp. 6, 7.

220. *Ibid.*, p. 7.

for the preaching of hell. First, God commands it and it is essential for a steward to be found faithful to his charge. But, second, God ordains such preaching because the sottish sinner is not interested in the fruits of the Spirit. Therefore, third, he must be shown the danger of his present condition and the impending doom that is hanging over his head. However, fourth, the actual sight of hell would be more than frail man could stand, so only the dim pictures found in the biblical warnings are suitable to awakening. But, fifth, awakening to a state of fear does not take a man out of his natural condition, and though he be desperately frightened, as the devils are, his most importunate prayers (if motivated merely by a sinful self-interest) still offend God, but not so much as their absence. Sixth, and this is the crucial point, in this awakened condition, operating only from self-interest, the sinner may (and the preacher encourages him) ask, "What must I do to be saved?" The answer to that question is not, "Be scared straight" but, "Believe on the Lord Jesus Christ and thou shalt be saved." But, finally, true faith in Christ is not a mere desperate or nominal acceptance of him, as a ticket out of hell, but a genuine, affectionate trust in him for the very loveliness and excellency of his being. This true faith, to be sure, is not in man's present disposition, but he may and must seek for a new birth from above.

It would be a great mistake, we note in conclusion, to suppose that Edwards preached hell and nothing but hell to unawakened sinners. While he thought that this was the doctrine most likely to awaken them from their corruptions, he also appealed to their love of pleasure. All men want to cultivate pleasure as well as avoid pain. They can be appealed to from either angle. There is no doubt that Edwards believed there was more likelihood of success awakening sottish sinners to their danger from where they were going than from what they were missing.

The Objections to Hell

". . . notwithstanding the plausibility of . . . objections, the principle of such thoughts . . . is a want of a sense of the horrible evil of sin."

Edwards has said that the only way men can endure even the thought of hell in this world is to deny hell in the hereafter. But man cannot live by denials. He must put out the future fires even for present peace of mind. This is, to use R. C. Sproul's expression, "the psychology of atheism."[221]

At one time or another, Edwards faces virtually every objection ever raised against endless punishment. How could God have created men destined for such an awful end? Does not the extremity of the punishment violate the elemental principle of justice, not to mention mercy? Does not this behavior—God inflicting eternal torture on his enemies—run contrary to the ethical law he impresses on his creatures of *loving* their enemies?

How could God create men destined for endless suffering? When Edwards addresses this objection he acknowledges its cogency and then proceeds not really to answer it.

> It is much to be suspected, that notwithstanding the plausibleness of such an objection, the very principal reason of such thoughts arising in the mind is a want of a sense of the horrible evil of sin. This disposes us to pity the damned wretch and that disposes [us] to look back and reflect upon the Author of his being and orderer of his misery because we haven't sense enough of the evil of sin to stir up indignation enough in us against it to balance the horror that arises from a sense of the dreadfulness of his suffering. This makes us pity the sufferer and this raises objections against God. . . .

(He continues with the already cited reference, by contrast, to Antiochus Epiphanes, whose wickedness we do see and whose endless sufferings Edwards thinks he and we can accept.)[222]

Edwards is answering the objection in terms of what man has become—a sinner—rather than the terms in which the objection was raised—why would God create a person destined to become a sinner deserving eternal suffering? God, in Edwards's theology, could have avoided creating such—why didn't he? God could have prevented sin entering the world—why didn't he? God could have redeemed these suffering sinners at no extra redemptive cost—why didn't he? Strange that Edwards misses the point here while he answers it elsewhere when the question is not being

---

221. *The Psychology of Atheism* (Minneapolis: Bethany Fellowship, Inc., 1974).
222. M866.

asked. He makes it very plain that the purpose hell serves is to gladden heaven. Suffering sinners serve the purpose of contributing to the bliss of redeemed sinners by glorifying the justice of God, as we have seen. Edwards seems not to be able quite to say that God originally decreed their creation for that purpose. "All things are yours [elect]," he had observed in reference to hell. Hell would never have been, apart from the divine purpose. Implicitly, therefore, Edwards is saying that God ordained, by permissive decree, reprobates for misery for the greater happiness of the elect. He seems unable to state the grim facts that harshly. So he points out the suitableness of sinners for suffering rather than why God created them and ordained them to that dread, though deserved, end.

Does not the extremity of an infinite punishment for finite sinners not violate the elemental principle of justice? Here again though he deals with this as a rationale for hell, Edwards fails to answer the objection (as stated) which he dealt with often elsewhere. Note here in M491 his phrasing of the objection followed by an answer to a different question, so uncharacteristic of our meticulous theologian.

> Some may be ready to think that it's incredible that God should bring miseries upon a creature that are so extreme and amazing and also eternal and desperate. But the dreadfulness and extremity of it is no argument against it, for those that are damned are entirely lost and utterly thrown away by God. As to any sort of regard that he has to their welfare their existence is for nothing else but to suffer.

This amounts to saying that God punishes them because he has no use for them—he could not care less for them. Even so, the question asks, Is God not unfair in punishing them so inordinately, so extremely? This answer does not refute that charge; if anything, it substantiates it. For Edwards's real answer we must go back to his proof cited above that infinite punishment is really finite as apprehended by the creature and that the finite creature deserves all he receives because of his sin against an infinitely excellent and divine person.

The most excruciating question rising against endless torment is, of course, how it could come from a being of infinite mercy. Here Edwards is woefully inadequate. How can hell consist with the merciful nature of God? he asks. Responding without answering, he says that the saints in heaven will not be shocked by the sufferings of hell. They have a livelier apprehension of the guilt of these sinful sufferers and their great enmity against God. Therefore, "it will seem no way cruel in God to inflict such extreme sufferings on such extremely wicked creatures."[223] What has become of the question, not to mention the mercy of God? Sin and suffering is the occasion for mercy, not an explanation of its absence. Sin has been as great and greater in many of the elect on whom God had exercised mercy than in some of the reprobates, as Edwards often observes. Why does the presence of such obnoxiousness explain why mercy is impossible? Edwards is so obviously irrational in answering these questions that one wonders if he was so torn apart himself that it boggled his own usually clear mind. Normally, Edwards gives a straightforward and traditional answer that God is sovereign in his mercy, as we have seen, having mercy on whom he will have mercy according to his great wisdom and purpose. If mercy were not sovereign, God would be at the mercy of sinners. But gazing right into the fires of hell must have blinded Edwards himself.

Edwards returns to his clear-headedness when he deals with the objection that God behaves differently in hating and punishing his enemies than when he commands his followers to love and befriend their enemies. Five solid reasons (which we have considered above) are given for the resolution of this apparent ethical paradox.

Edwards has one basic answer to the objectors to eternal hell: They do not understand the infinite sinfulness of sin; the infinity of heinousness in wickedness.

The Accursed Vision

"God will be hell."

Is there anything in Edwards's doctrine of hell that corresponds to the beatific vision of heaven? That is difficult to say.

---

223. M558.

If there is the counterpart of the beatific vision it would obviously have to be its mirror image or opposite. In the beatific vision the saints see God in himself, as he is, so far as they are capable. The veil is drawn aside for a moment and man for that moment "sees God." "Blessed are the pure in heart for they shall see God."

Is the exact opposite the case with sinners? Not really. In fact, the exact same is the case with sinners! They too, at times, see God in his essence, as we have shown earlier. But what they see is God's essence as a consuming fire. The same God whom the saints see as their supreme lover, sinners see as the enemy of their souls. The divine and supernatural light of the saint is the divine and supernatural darkness of the sinner. One is the vision that beatifies indeed; the other curses. As the redeemed see God as the source of every blessing that heaven affords, the impenitent see God as the source of every curse of hell. He is behind the enmity of their former friends. It is he who does not incite, but does direct, the malice of the devils toward the wicked victims. The sinner's own conscience, the internal tormentor, is but God pushing outward. For the saint, heaven is God. For the wicked, hell is God. Cursed are the impure in heart for they too shall see God!

Conclusion

Modern Christian theology has tended to take either the pain out of eternity or the eternity out of pain. Perhaps the best way to show this gradual departure from Jonathan Edwards (and Jesus Christ!) is to note the theology of A. H. Strong. This eminent scholar was one of the three greats of the turn of our century along with Charles Hodge and W. G. T. Shedd (all of them reformed theologians). The concluding section of his incredibly learned three-volume *Systematic Theology*[224] deals with hell.

While calmly and firmly avowing adherence to the orthodox doctrine, though in conscious pain because of its sensed unpopu-

---

224. Philadelphia: Judson Press, 1917.

larity, Strong does essentially and possibly unconsciously take the suffering out of eternity or the eternity out of the suffering. Affirming hell he denies its hellishness. This avowed friend of the doctrine is the actual enemy. And there can be no doubt that advocates of hell like this did more to put out its fires than all its real enemies could do.

"Summing it all up," Strong writes, "we may say, it [hell] is the loss of all good, whether physical or spiritual, and the misery of an evil conscience banished from God and from the society of the holy, and dwelling under God's positive curse forever." After listening to Edwards one would ask: This is hell? One must remember again that Strong was one of the biblical doctrine's major champions a century and a half after Edwards's death.

The implications of Strong's position are quite obvious, but he does not leave us to implications.

> We freely concede: 1. that future pain does not necessarily consist of physical torment . . . ; 2. that the pain and suffering of the future are not necessarily due to positive inflictions of God—they may result entirely from the soul's sense of loss and from the accusations of conscience; and 3. that eternal punishment does not necessarily involve endless successions of suffering—as God's eternity is not mere endlessness, so we may not be forever subject to the law of time.[225]

There is the doctrine of hell with hell left out.

As a footnote to this essential regression from the orthodox doctrine by an orthodox man, several lesser items are worth noticing. In this discussion God's permissive decrees are never related to damnation, though Strong was a Calvinist. Edwards's conversion turned on this point. The fewness of the lost is conspicuous as Strong approvingly cites the other two great Calvinists of the time, Shedd and Hodge (who say that the lost compare in number as the inmates of a prison to the general community). Edwards shows throughout that the relative fewness of numbers describes not the lost but the saved. Again, Strong falls far below Edwards in the role he gives to fear: "The fear of a future punishment, though not the highest motive, is yet a proper mo-

---

225. *Ibid.*, p. 1035.

tive.''[226] We have shown that that kind of fear is not a proper motive at all except to awaken people to their need for the only proper motive, which is love. In his earnest effort to avoid ''scare theology'' Strong falls into it while it was Edwards who avoided it. The treatment of God's relation to hell is the saddest of all Strong's defections. For Edwards, God's presence was the real torment of hell (just as his presence was the blessing of heaven) while for Strong ''the pains and suffering of the future are not necessarily due, to the positive inflictions of God.'' Of course, Strong and others would no doubt say, ''We do not mean that God is absent except in his love.'' This will not do, because when one equates God's absence with the absence of God's love, one is defining God exclusively as love. Therein is the greatest error of our times into which Jonathan Edwards never fell. God is love but he is more than love and he is other than love. God is holiness; God is justice; God is wisdom; God is wrath. God is God.

It is no wonder that one of the most outstanding conservative theologians of our own day (who may be the contemporary A. H. Strong in his vastness of learning and acumen), Bernard Ramm, in his *Handbook of Contemporary Theology*[227] has no entries at all under hell (or even heaven). How Edwards would weep if he were not in the place where all tears are wiped away.

Edwards never tired of describing, proving, demonstrating, and preaching endless heaven, endless hell. But there can be no doubt where his heart was. Even as he defended ''the justice of God in the damnation of sinners'' he triumphantly extolled the divine and everlasting mercy in the salvation of saints. Jonathan Edwards was in his truest element not as the faithful, fiery preacher of ''sinners in the hands of an angry God''—though this he ever was and ever remained—but as the rhapsodic seer of the ''beatific vision.''

---

226. *Ibid.*, p. 1055.
227. Grand Rapids: Eerdmans Publishing Co., 1966.

$\frac{15}{76}$ Arguments for the eternity of Hell

P 78 understanding eternal punishment.
       (entire page)